JUNG

and Shakespeare

JUNG

and Shakespeare

HAMLET, OTHELLO, AND THE TEMPEST

BARBARA ROGERS-GARDNER

Chiron Publications • Wilmette, Illinois

Second printing, 1996

The Chiron Monograph Series, Volume VII
General Editors: Nathan Schwartz-Salant and Murray Stein
Managing Editor: Siobhan Drummond

Grateful acknowledgement is made for permission to reprint quotations from the following copyrighted material:
The Collected Works of C. G. Jung, published by Princeton University Press, 1956.
Shakespeare and the Ambiguity of Love's Triumph by Charles Lyons, published by Mouton de Gruyter, 1971.
Psyche and Symbol in Shakespeare by Alex Aronson, published by Harvard University Press, 1972.
The Masks of God: Creative Mythology by Joseph Campbell, published by Penguin, USA, 1968.
The Critic Agonistes: Psychology, Myth, and the Art of Fiction by Daniel Weiss, copyright 1985, University of Washington Press.
Identity: Youth and Crisis by Erik Erikson, published by W.W. Norton & Company, Inc., 1968.
Origins and History of Consciousness by Erich Neumann, published by Princeton University Press, 1970.

Permissions continued on page 118.

I would like to thank Thao Luong for his technical help with manuscript preparation.

Library of Congress Catalog Number: 91–27361

Printed in the United States of America.
Cover design by Michael Barron.
Book design by Siobhan Drummond.

Library of Congress Cataloging-in-Publication Data

Rogers-Gardner, Barbara J., 1935–
    Jung and Shakespeare / Barbara J. Rogers-Gardner.
        p. cm. — (The Chiron monograph series ; v. 7)
    Includes bibliographical references and index.
    ISBN 0–933029–55–1 : $12.95
        1. Shakespeare, William, 1564–1616—Knowledge—Psychology.
    2. Jung, C. G. (Carl Gustav), 1875–1961—Views on literature.
    3. Archetype (Psychology) in literature. 4. Psychoanalysis and
    literature. I. Title. II. Series.
    PR3065.R64 1992
    822.3'3—dc20   91–27361
                                                                        CIP

ISBN 0–933029–55–1

For my husband, Mark

Contents

Introduction

"Shakespeare had a dream—and we are it."
C. G. Jung

"We are such stuff as dreams are made on."
Shakespeare, *The Tempest*

Jung understood that during the process of creation, artists are caught up in a mystery, writhing in the womb of myth. The artist brings his story from the dream-state into the conscious structure of language, which is never precisely adequate to the vision it holds. "A great work of art is like a dream," Jung wrote, "for all its apparent obviousness, it does not explain itself and is always ambiguous" (*CW* 15,104/161).[1] The symbolic content of both poetry and dream is drawn from the innate, transpersonal images of the collective unconscious (*CW* 15,80-1/126-7,104/161). From that source, the poet expresses what T. S. Eliot called "the deeper, unnamed feelings which form the substratum of our being."[2] To analyze a work of literature, for Jung, was to look beneath the accidents of plot and character, seeking the symbolic pattern of the work, whether or not it was known to the artist.

Authors of what Jung called "psychological" works shape their material consciously and so were of less interest to him than were "visionary" poets like Shakespeare. Such an artist may hide "visionary experience in a cloak of historical or mythical events, which are then erroneously taken to be the real subject matter" (*CW* 15,91/143). The plot for Jung was only the vehicle for meaning. The meaning itself is found in what Aristotle called "action" and Dante the "moto spiritale," that is, in the divine moral/spiritual order working itself out on the small human stage. Literature thus becomes more than an aesthetically and intellectually pleasing arrangement of words, but an avenue into the collective unconscious that would otherwise remain what A.C. Bradley called tragedy—a "painful mystery." Drama becomes the healing event Aristotle believed it was, offering a catharsis of destructive emotions and a means of uniting the outer life with the inner one, the material world with the spiritual world. I make no apologies for referring in these pages to the spiritual aspect of human life. We live in times too terrible to ignore it. Shakespeare does not only offer material for academic grants and doctoral theses, but a model for healing the sick modern soul. We need every such model we can get.

Far from being the symptom of neurosis Freud thought it was, the act of art was for Jung a way to integrate the chaotic instincts into the order of consciousness. Jung's "visionary artist" is taken over by a larger purpose than his own conscious one, much the way Prospero's revenge is forgotten in the forgiveness prompted by Ariel, his transpersonal spirit. The artist does not so much create his or her vision but is re-created by it, as is the audience. The greater the work of art, the more the artist has stood aside from it and let the personal diminish in the light of the transpersonal. Ben Jonson, fastidious tinker of dead plays, wished Shakespeare had blotted a thousand lines, instead of scribbling without a backward look. For Jung, however, the less the artist tries to control the birth of a visionary work, the better chance for life it has.

Art is an instinct, an autonomous complex, in that it cannot be willed, and the frenzy in which it is produced is more divine than pathological. Jung says the psychologist, like the critic, must "break down life and events. . .into meanings, images, concepts," losing the "living mystery" of art in the process (*CW* 15,78/121). He did not believe psychologists could replace literary critics, or that psychological analysis was a substitute for aesthetic analysis: "It is an important principle of psychology that any given psychic material can be shown to derive from causal antecedents; it is a principle of aesthetics that a psychic product can be regarded as existing in and for itself" (*CW* 15,87/135). The two methods of analysis complement each other.

Jung would not have us psychoanalyze literary characters as if they were patients, for we might thereby lose the larger symbolic patterns of the play, along with the mythic dimension, and the beauty of the medium—metered metaphoric language. The assumption by Freudians is that art is a neurotic symptom and is made out of the artist's pain, like a pearl by an oyster. Jung more credibly linked art to dream, although dream lacks the logic, morality, form, consistency, and sense of great art. In the end, Jung's metaphor falters too, as all metaphors do, when nose to nose with life.

As art begins in the unconscious of the artist, criticism must start from the same place in the critic. It must address not the personal quirks, problems, and limitations of the artist, but the symbolic content of the work itself. Jung suggests that criticism, to be of any use, must arise from the collective unconscious, from the mythic and primordial images that shape the instinctive expression of the human race. Although we have no inborn ideas, we are predisposed to "inborn possibilities of ideas" and these figure our fantasies, reminding us that we grow out of significant, ancestral soil. We participate in the primitive experience through archetypes, which evoke our personal and collective past.

Jung says of archetypes that they "resemble dry river beds to which water may return at any time" (*CW* 10,189/395). Maud Bodkin, echoing Jung, calls such an archetype in poetry: "a particular form or pattern which persists amid variation from age to age, and which corresponds to a pattern or configuration of emotional tendencies in the minds of those who are stirred by the theme."[3] Isolating and clarifying the archetypal situation in the play cannot be the whole of dramatic analysis, for archetypes are permanent and drama, as every critic since Aristotle has recognized, is about change.

We cannot look only at the "typicality of the action" and neglect the "complex and ambiguous use of it in the poem."[4] The same caveat applies to myth and ritual, which Jung suggests are the substratum of great literature. Myth is only potentially the kind of narrative found in a Shakespearean tragedy.[5] Ritual is only potentially art, for ritual is a sacred pattern strictly followed, while art overflows such limits and becomes more ambiguous and complex as it departs from ritual, that is, from the archetypal pattern.[6]

Without this ambiguity and complexity, art is a tinkling cymbal, a row of Andy Warhol's tomato soup cans. Jung's aesthetic theory allows for a work of art that does not merely sort and arrange the self-serving notions of the day, but one that erupts, past cleverness and caution, into a new heaven and a new earth. Shakespeare's plays are just such visionary art. To receive them, we must close the books and open the heart. "We are such stuff as dreams are made on and our little life is rounded with a sleep." Let us learn what we can, while we can. To become lovers instead of scientists is a hard injunction to the scholars who have made reputations on proper academic readings of a poet who cared so little for propriety that he never edited his plays nor made a clean, authoritative version of them.

The three plays chosen for analysis reflect crucial points in human development, as seen from a psychoanalytic perspective. In *Hamlet*, a son fights free of his parents, and in his struggle acts out the birth of the ego. In *Othello*, male and female attempt a union which is blighted by a conflict between anima and animus. In *The Tempest*, Prospero successfully undergoes the process of individuation and faces his imminent death with full acceptance, knowing that "waxing and waning make one curve" (*CW* 8,407/800). Not in individualism, the maladaptive bog in which Claudius, Iago, and Stephano sink, but in accommodating the self to the social order, does the Shakespearean hero find his peace. The dying Desdemona does not complain of her fate but exonerates Othello of guilt. She and Prospero end in a state of Jungian grace—with their consciousness and their consciences clear. They end complete. For Jung, tragedy was essentially invalid, for all psychic change is a kind of death. By the final scene, Shakespeare's heroes, with the possible exception of Macbeth and King Lear, know that "ripeness is all." In death, they discover a goal from which it is unhealthy to shrink, for such a shrinking "robs the second half of life of its purpose" (*CW* 6,402/792).

As the dark mystery of death is confronted, archetypes surface and demand to be acknowledged, if the human person is to become whole and wise. Archetypes do not walk about on the stage, for their very essence is hiddenness. Once they are made conscious, they are no longer archetypes, but characters, partaking more or less in the qualities of a particular archetype. A model of Jung's mature, harmonious self is to be found in Prospero's gentle trust that death was an initiation into divinity. The anima is realized in Desdemona's unconditional love of Othello. Prospero's shadow is recognized and embraced in Caliban, the poetic, sensual monster who grounds us in pignuts and music.

An introduction to Shakespeare and Jung might be scholarly and academic. This one is not. The only intention of the author is to draw together two wise men, who knew human nature at the root, for readers who know that they knew.

Chapter One

Hamlet

Some years ago anthropologist Laura Bohannan sat with a primitive tribe in New Guinea around the evening campfire. Everyone had to tell a story to entertain and instruct the tribe, and she cast about for a story universal enough to suit any culture. *Hamlet* was her choice. She started with the ghost, at which tribesmen rolled their eyes and whispered to each other that the ghost was no good. Ghosts are never any good and Hamlet shouldn't listen to this one. Bohannan tried to explain that the ghost was an honest ghost, but she had to admit that he came from hell. Next she told them that Uncle Claudius had married Hamlet's mother. The tribesmen murmured again, this time approvingly, since a proper tribal man must marry his brother's widow. They thought Hamlet a fool and Claudius a hero. The desperate anthropologist concluded her story with the final bloodbath, in which Hamlet gets revenge. Clucking his disapproval, the chief said, "What a mess. No longer any king. Everybody's dead, and it's all Hamlet's fault. Listen to ghosts and you'll wind up one of them." The anthropologist's story had fallen flat. Apparently the universality of *Hamlet* is by no means obvious, even to the accomplished storytellers of New Guinea. A psychoanalytic reading of the play, therefore, is only one cautious possibility, and that caveat should be remembered.

To start with, it must be said that Hamlet is not your easiest patient. He's a mystery, going from euphoria to depression in two lines. One minute he says man is like a god, and the next he's calling man "this quintessence of dust." It would cost any therapist a groaning to take off his edge. Hamlet's mystery is traceable to the conflicting archetypes he struggles to contain and reconcile in the course of the play—particularly the wise old father and the seductive, devouring mother.

For both Jung and Jacques Lacan, a contemporary Freudian literary analyst, the unconscious is the ultimate source of art. Unlike Jung, Lacan sees no point in chasing archetypes around the room, since if we caught one, it would dissolve in our hands like old Hamlet's Ghost at dawn. Lacan's symbols have no absolute identity and so differ from the archetypes. In his rather disappointing piece on *Hamlet*, Lacan is strictly Freudian, assuming that what's really at issue in the whole play is who wears the phallus.[1] Hamlet is ambivalent about the matter, seeing Lacan's desired, impossible-to-win Other not as the phallus but as union with nourishing bliss, what Lacan, and his predecessor Ernest Jones, recognizes elsewhere as the mother. She in herself isn't the object of his desire, which is both for love and for death. She is only the symbol of it.

Hamlet is more the mystic than the warrior, less interested in either possessing a phallus or taking someone else's, than in re-experiencing the love and connectedness that he once had with his mother, the love that he tries to regain with Rosencrantz and Guildenstern and that he enjoys with Horatio. Or, expressed another way, Hamlet's desire is to school himself in wisdom, among philosophic men, not drunken yahoos like the types who live at Elsinore. Hamlet-the-child wants two contradictory things: 1) a functioning ego like that of Claudius, an ego that will allow him to do his manly duty and pacify the Ghost and 2) ego-death in oceanic bliss with his mother. What Hamlet-the-adult wants, we get only a glimpse of, but it seems to be what Jung would call maturation, successful separation from the family, ability to love, and ability to accept both one's divinity and one's mortality.

The problem of the play is that Hamlet's desire for philosophic peace and wisdom is at war with his duty to avenge his father. It's an assignment that would make John Wayne sob in his pillow. Hamlet's duty is to become a man, leave the world of women and avenge his Oedipal loss by murdering somebody. The Ghost says to murder Claudius, but the idea is just murder. Of anybody. André Gide wrote that a man who has not killed is a virgin, as Hamlet is until he kills Polonius. Lacan is right when he says that what Hamlet really lacked, until the Ghost appeared, is a goal, that is to say, he lacked a masculine agenda and has been living in the moment, like a child or traditional woman, surrendering to whatever comes along. In fact he is always at the mercy of some other man's agenda, sent here and there, punished, manipulated into fighting. In the end, he kills with a borrowed sword. Yet Lacan comes short of saying that Hamlet is more comfortable in the world of women than in the world of men, which is the argument here.

Despite his Freudian obsession with the phallus—who has one, who wants one, who would kill to get one—Lacan has some affinities with Jung. For one thing, Lacan's ubiquitous phallus is not a physical thing but a signifier of life, a symbol. Even Ophelia, Lacan says, is a symbol of the lost phallus, which is why Hamlet goes after her, both in love and

---

6

hate. Hamlet continually talks of conception when Ophelia is in his neighborhood. He sends her to a nunnery, Elizabethan slang for brothel, and at the play he stages, wants to lie in her lap, joking about the nothing that lies between a maid's legs. Later, Ophelia drowns herself among water plants known as "dead men's fingers," after singing some bawdy songs. Clearly, Lacan has a point. In his view, Hamlet has been deprived of his Father, i.e., his phallus. He therefore desires Ophelia, the object which replaces the thing he needed, and which he is unconscious of needing. Yet if Hamlet is after power, Ophelia was certainly the last place to go for it. Ophelia is only a replacement for someone else whom he is also unconscious of needing: his mother and the worldview she represents.

Hamlet is often accused of being too intellectual, frozen by thought into inaction. But is he? He certainly has not thought out a plan to kill the king. He merely muddles through events, living from moment to moment. He is a visionary, a seer, a poet, somebody who thinks in symbols, paradoxes, and graphic images.[2] Other characters talk like textbooks, like the windbags of earlier Elizabethan drama, including Shakespeare's. With the character of Hamlet, Shakespeare brings onto the stage for the first time a complete personality with a new language, trying on roles, playing the madman, trying to get a grip on a new world—the inner world as it abrades the outer, where metaphor and language are born. Hamlet refers the general to the particular, often the grubby particular. Othello likes to be cosmic and wave his arms about, while Hamlet consistently uses black comedy, mocking himself, reducing the grand to the ordinary. To Claudius, he says, "I eat the air, promise-cramm'd. You cannot feed capons so." He refers to himself as a eunuch, a fat, emasculated chicken. He is not a fairy tale prince, or even a typical Elizabethan hero.

Compared to Hamlet, other characters seem part of a dumb-show. He is universal, one of us, beamed down on an Elizabethan stage by accident. It's easier for us to get into his skin than into King Lear's or Macbeth's. It's easier to see him as a patient. Everybody does, from Freud to Lacan. That's because he's more than a hero; he's everybody's childhood and youth.

If Hamlet is a hero on his way toward separation from the parents, he could also be seen as Lacan's infant, initially unable to separate his elemental images from his very being. They are a sort of fantasy bank, from which all later symbols, language, and art are borrowed. When the infant learns words, Lacan says, he is merely displacing references to a repressed other (m-Other) by metonymy, an unstated absent idea or object. Jung explains the structure of the soul as "already present, the pre-condition. It is the mother (*CW* 43, 236 f)." The mother, for Jung, is not merely a walking womb, but a symbol for the unitive, mystical life.

Let's backtrack a bit, going to analyst critics before Lacan. What did they do with the feminine in Hamlet? Critics like Freud and Ernest Jones tried to tidy up the excess that we see in Hamlet's reactions. They call him a melancholic, a hysteric, and think a neat oedipal reading of the play, a mere diagnosis, solves this hero's riddle. Freud and Jones, like T. S. Eliot, for different reasons, want no esthetic excess, no irrationality contaminating the final analysis. The work of art must explain every aspect of the character, turn id into ego, as Freud put it. Yet Freud was aware that Hamlet raises more problems than he or his analyst can solve. In "Mourning and Melancholia" (1915), Freud suggested that the line between rationality and excess breaks down when "the melancholic is defined as a madman who also speaks the truth." Serpieri amplifies Freud's as follows:

> We can only wonder why a man has to be ill before he can be accessible to a truth of this kind. For there can be no doubt that if anyone holds an opinion of himself such as this (an opinion which Hamlet holds of himself and everyone else) he is ill. . .[3]

He believed that in Hamlet, "it can of course be only the poet's mind which confronts us," and assumed that Shakespeare himself had a mother complex that obliged him to marry a much older woman. Freud admitted, "I have found love of the mother and jealousy of the father in my own case too," so perhaps his obsession with Hamlet says more about his own problem than Shakespeare's.

The trouble with seeing art as a symptom is that we tend to diagnose characters, reducing them to their own shadows, instead of accepting their mysterious wholeness. Jaques in *As You Like It* thus becomes an involutional, Hamlet a manic-depressive, and Desdemona a masochist. Jung, instead, stressed the symbolic content of the work of art rather than dwelling exclusively on the neurotic behavior of individual characters, or, worse yet, of the author, running them through mazes of diagnosis as if they were so many rats. Reductive oedipalism does not explain Hamlet, nor does the archetype of the hero slaying the family dragon, though both may illuminate a piece of the action.

Freud saw Hamlet as one of those neurotic characters who brought out the neurotic in the spectator, breaking down habitual mental barriers. The hope of traditional analysts is that the problem of Hamlet and of us all can rationally be solved, if not in the hero, then by turning to spectator and critic and curing them, or at least making them conscious of their Hamlet-like desire for the mother and identification with her. The assumption of such a reading is that our psychosexual problems can be neatly identified and resolved. Since we can never rationally determine what is fantasy, the assumption is flawed. Yet the mystery of Hamlet's problem leaks into the margins, overrunneth the cup. Jones threw up his hands and saw the excess as intractable femininity itself. Eliot, also fed up with mystery, said Gertrude simply wasn't reason enough for Hamlet to turn distraught. Psychoanalytic critics generally have resisted the feminine in Hamlet, but the wind is shifting.

Femininity is seen by some recent psychoanalytic critics as "the very basis of the aesthetic process."[4] If it is, Hamlet, in a fatal move, simultaneously shuts down the feminine in himself, aborting his intuitive, compassionate aspect, when he insults the femininity of Ophelia and Gertrude. André Green thinks Shakespeare used the play to reconcile male and female in himself, making the feminine respectable by equating it with aesthetic creation. Both Green and Winnicott, like Jung, see creation rising out of that mysterious, primordial inner space in all of us, the space that is metaphorically female, and which does not yet have a subject/object relationship, because there is no self to be related *to*. It is the side of us that does not yet have a language, or whose language has begun to break down under the pressure of experience. Creation begins at the point before signs or words begin to separate and categorize experience. The creative act, then, originates in what Lacan calls the "metonymic stage" of psychological development. Instead of the classical, traditional notion that the source of art is form, metaphor, structure—in Lacan's metaphoric world of the fathers—these new psychoanalytic critics are suggesting that art begins in the unconscious, in the feminine. They all use Hamlet to prove their point, but then everybody uses Hamlet to prove a point.

Lacan calls the infant Hamlet "l'hommelette," infant man with no boundaries, or broken egg, with mixed yoke and white. The hero is a little ham, a born actor who prefers acting to statecraft, any day. This infant starts to sense a gap between his desire (mother) and the intruder Claudius, who represents prohibition, taboo, law, separation, and is in general bad news. Lacan, with Freud, calls this pain of loss castration and sees it internalized as the father principle, with its public prestige. Opposing Lacan's "metaphoric mode" is the mother principle, which represents the private, personal world which Lacan calls "metonymic." The mythical Sphinx asked Oedipus, Hamlet's prototype, "What is man?" while the modern Hamlet asks Lacan's question: "What am I here in my parents' discourse?" Remember, the Sphinx kills whoever can't get the answer.

Once "l'hommelette" asks this question, acknowledging the split between himself and his perception of Mother and World, he's in trouble. Lacan sees the split as part of an imbalance occurring between a forgotten, lost pre-conscious experience and his new naming ability. To pull himself together, Hamlet, like all of us, then invents words, words, words, trying to bandage the gap between body perceptions and what we call the "Real" situation, that is substituting "real" names for lost, unknown ones. Like Hamlet, we're all trying to fill up the gap of infant experience, creating a world with an act of art. We fool ourselves into thinking that this world is "real."

Hamlet pretends madness and creates theater, holding up mirrors to everyone but himself. He's like Nietzsche's idealist, a "creature who has reasons for remaining in the dark about himself, and is clever enough to remain in the dark about these reasons." Hamlet gets poor forty-something Gertrude under a cruel blue fluorescent light, the depressing kind they have in public bathrooms, the kind that would make even Helen of Troy look like she needed a face lift, and what does he do? He holds up a mirror. Now poor Gertrude has been partying a lot, drinking more akvavit than she can gracefully handle, and Hamlet has made her cry. So besides being hung over, she has a red nose, and her mascara is running. That's when Hamlet forces her to look in the mirror. This moment when the mirror is held up is a metaphorical death, an acting out of the moment when the gap opens between our first body perceptions and the "Real," that is, the named Experience. All language, symbols, and theater do is try to cope with the split.

Hamlet has fallen between real and fantasy, metonymy and meta-phor, mother and father, and is a hero controlling nothing. He's a student who'd like to go back to grad school, and if the king would just give him his papers, he'd go. "Hamlet's the best example of the fact that many dramatic crises can be avoided by the prompt issuance of pass-ports," Lacan remarks. "If Hamlet had been given his papers to travel to Wittenberg, there would have been no drama."⁵ Hamlet stays at home *because his mother asks him to.* He is caught in the web of mater-nal love, the labyrinth with a monster at its heart. Though he is the most articulate and conscious of Shakespeare's heroes, Hamlet, following the pattern of the hero's journey, begins as the infant hero fighting separation from the parent. His concern to defend his ego rationally during this separation is the theme of the play. All his stratagems—the Dumbshow, feigned madness—are like the myths and concepts we use to create absolute meaning where there can be none. The end of *King Lear* is just about as sad, except that at least the hero is old. A drama like *Hamlet* is similar in Lacan's view to a psychoanalytic session. Hamlet is all of us, at that point in our development where we break with primal unity and must begin to look for it in the symbolic language of art, under every bed, behind every closed door, and in the eyes of every lover for the rest of our lives.

Hamlet is also a representative of the Renaissance, that childhood of our own era, full of idealism, energy, and contradiction, as childhoods are. Along with the idealism, which we see in Hamlet's adoration of real men—his father and Fortinbras—the Renaissance was obsessed with decay or "mutability." If the ideal is father, the eternal one, then the opposite is earthly, natural decay and death, associated in Shakespeare and Jung with the mother. We have seen how Hamlet refers to the two-sided nature of man as both divine and "this quintessence of dust." His idea of nature roughly resembles a toxic waste dump; nature is like women and death—terrifying and uncontrollable. He doesn't trust his natural impulses, telling Ophelia to get to a nunnery before he loses control of himself and becomes as bad as other men, meaning Claudius. He is like the hero of those movies in which a modest scientist warns his beloved that owing to having drunk a malevolent potion, he is about to turn into a beast. From such rapid shifts in his diction, we can hear Hamlet acting out in speech the agony of his original split from the mother, that is, from that aspect of himself which is unified, unconscious, primitive, and, as Dr. Ruth would put it, capable of Terrific Sex. Hamlet has learned to think, no doubt at graduate school, and his life is ruined. The renaissance ideal of education was perhaps at fault here. Fear of disorder and decay had made the Elizabethans insistent on decorum, order, and self-knowledge, meaning self-control. The function of literature was no longer to praise God or celebrate nature in myth, but to make solid, sensible subjects for a totalitarian ruler. The idea was, give the kids good literature to read and they will become virtuous, obedient, and useful. *Dulcis et utile.* It was like sitting Charles Manson down to read Milton's *Paradise Lost* and expecting him to go out and feed the homeless. Without self-knowledge, such admonitions are useless, as Montaigne recognized, and Montaigne was the chief source for Hamlet's philosophy.

All through the play Hamlet looks to others for identity, for knowledge of himself, and fails to find it. When he compares himself to others, he can suffer only pain and humiliation. Ultimately, philosophic abstractions do not solve his problem; only what Jung calls maturation can do that, and Hamlet runs out of time before maturation can occur. By Act V, he speaks sad, noble, stoical lines that echo the new Elizabethan skepticism, born of classicism and a fear that entropy, not God, was in charge of the world. Iago and Antonio, in later plays, carry this skepticism into nihilism. Perhaps Hamlet saw that shift coming when he said, "The rest is silence." Iago echoes these sentiments when he's at the end of the line. Ironically, the two characters who are most alike in all of Shakespeare are the beloved Hamlet and Iago, the villain everyone loves to hate. The shadow-criminal, as Jung would put it, is the unacknowledged side of the noble idealist.

For our patriarchal culture, the crime that made law codes necessary is parricide. Lacan suggests that the only full-fledged myth to enter our historical age is Freud's version of the Oedipus story. The primordial crime is necessarily followed by the historical legal system designed to prevent the crime's recurrence. Parricide, for Freud, is the origin of the horde and the law at the start of the Judaic tradition, that is, at the beginning of the Western code of justice. Recall the early Greek myth of Chronos, the Titan who castrated his father Uranus with a sickle, chopped him into messes, then took his place. Chronos, by the way, was protected by his mother. To escape his bad karma, he tried to remain childless, so no son of his would ever do to him what he had done to Uranus. So he ate all his children, until his wife hid Zeus, her youngest. Zeus, of course, grew up to send Chronos to his eternal sleep and took over the family business. The myth does not deal with his guilt, if he had any, but that guilt is at the heart of tragedy.

Every tragedy, a specifically Western form of art, is the renewal of such primal guilt and expiation. Every baptism, or ritual death, guarantees redemption or rebirth. First is the desire to kill the parent and from this desire comes transcendence of that guilty need—murder—the ultimate in separation from the parent. Lacan says, "the ideal father is the dead father."[6] *Hamlet*, Lacan points out, is about the crime of mothers and fathers, while Oedipus, in the Greek play, commits his own crime, not knowing what he does. In *Hamlet*, the crime is carried out deliberately, and by the villain, not by the hero. If the play has an oedipal action, it is that the Father, too, is an "Other," that is, this Ghost is no more in charge of truth or events than Hamlet is and is also castrated. In fact, that's what we hear the Ghost telling his son and what is so horrifying to Hamlet—if my mighty warrior-father couldn't get his life from plate to mouth, what chance have I, a mere "peasant slave?"

Tragedy, for the Freudians, is the art of making conscious the primal desire to kill the father. The play's the thing in which we catch our own conscience at its tricks, and begin to heal ourselves of deceit. Perhaps that's why Hamlet is forever asking people to be honest, that is, to be conscious.[7] He's like a therapist in action, both for himself and everybody else. His images and little digs unmask seemers, hypocrites like Rosencrantz, who is a "sponge that soaks up the king's countenance." Hamlet cuts Gertrude's heart in two while she's lying on her couch. When nobody's around to work over, he psychoanalyzes himself. He tries to figure out why he cannot murder the king, the father writ large. Hamlet, then, is a step beyond Oedipus, the first step toward solution of the problem. Hamlet's trouble is that though he came to accept death as part of life, he could not resolve his conflict because he never knew what it was.

Freud's point in 1924 was that the real oedipal mystery is not in the son's wish to kill his father and ravish his mother, *but that the desire is unconscious*. Once the desire has been made conscious and is mourned, the complex is in decline and on the way to being terminated. Lacan says: "If the process of genital maturation is to turn out well, the Oedipus complex must be terminated as completely as possible, for the consequence of this complex in both man and woman is the scar, the emotional stigma, of the castration complex."[8] Shakespeare critic Maynard Mack says much the same thing when he calls Hamlet a play about "the power of mortality," and that its three emphases are 1) human weakness and instability, 2) the infection or poison in human nature, and 3) loss.[9] His approach takes the play out of its oedipal procrustean bed and brings it closer to a Jungian symbolic reading, in which the loss mourned is within the individual, not merely an externally caused event. Acknowledging and accepting the loss is an archetypal issue, dependent on awareness of what has been killed inside the individual.

Jung's archetypes, as such, are not empirically represented on the stage. They are by definition the unconscious contents of the mind; to the soul they are "what instincts are to the body."[10] Myth gives us an archetype; the play gives the archetype a human face and the archetypal event both form and structure. So Hamlet may be the oedipal son, the anima-possessed hero, and the renaissance man of thought in rebellion against the violent warrior's world of the Middle Ages.

He may be all these things at once and more. We will not try to reduce him here to fit any paradigm, though the emphasis will be on the reluctant hero's duty to break from the "feminine order" of the heart and body, what Lacan calls "metonymy," in order to join the masculine order of mind, hierarchy, structure, or what Lacan calls the metaphoric mode. Hamlet is in a battle between mind and body, brains and feelings, dying and living. He must struggle his way out of the underworld, usually seen in myth as female. His mourning is the work of logos, according to Lacan, the culture's attempt to stuff the horrid hole left by death—that uncontrollable mystery. If the mourning rite, the healer of loss, is insufficient, and in this play it is, disorder in the kingdom and the psyche is inevitable.

An expiation is then necessary, and in *Hamlet,* Ophelia is the sacrificial lamb. When she's put in her grave, the last of Hamlet's humanity dies with her. Up to that point, he acts as if he could fix people and change things, like an adolescent who thinks it's enough to split with his parents and their hang-ups. Of course, now he's got to find a girl on whom to dump all his projections. Then, when she dies, he panics and jumps into her grave. Part of the awfulness of mourning is just this— we lose the person on whom we've projected all our problems, so we panic. We now have to take the burden on ourselves. And Hamlet does.

After the graveyard scene, Hamlet accepts the world as it is and himself as he is. The obsessional neurotic, according to Lacan, "sets up everything so that the object of his desire becomes the signifier of this impossibility," that is, of the attainment of the real object of desire.[11] Ophelia is thus a mere stand-in for Gertrude and what she archetypally represents. The trouble is, the more one desires the object, the more impossible is the possession of it. The myth of Tristan and Isolde's lovedeath is the medieval example of this hopeless feedback loop. Ophelia, for Hamlet, is only the signifier of impossible desire. He is going through the motions of love when he embraces her body and rants at her brother. When his mother, the ultimate recipient of his projections dies, Hamlet does more than playact. He both resists being born into maturity and longs for it; he both hates and loves his mother. If his father were still alive, he, too, would be hated as much as loved, for he would be another symbol of Hamlet's inability to fight free of family. Hamlet so exaggerates his love for the perfect, dead father that we can be sure of ambivalence and equivocal mourning. Since his father is dead, Hamlet can turn his fury only on Claudius, surrogate father and one with the mother (IV, ii, 51). We can only imagine what Hamlet's attitude toward his father was before the old king was murdered. Envy? Awe? Resentment? Certainly his encounter on the ramparts with his father's ghost was marked more by fear and reverence then by warmth and trust. Hamlet saves his jealous fury for Claudius, with whom he certainly had a history. This uncle—old enough to be Hamlet's father, young enough to be an older brother—had won all that to which Hamlet was heir before the play began. Sibling rivalry intensified the oedipal urge, and when we first see Hamlet, he is speechless with frustration, loss, and rage.

Claudius is behaving like the successful politician he is, aware that everyone supposes that he and Gertrude engaged in some hanky-panky over the meadbowl while old Hamlet was playing war games in Norway. He has thrown a good funeral for the brother he murdered, following it up with a party and conciliatory speeches, during which he attempts to please everybody and wraps himself in the flag. Claudius enjoys rituals, which have a calming effect on the state and on the conscience. He is no innovator or tormented self-analyst, and Hamlet can learn nothing from him except how not to be. Rather than following Claudius into a Machiavellian macho stance, Hamlet goes his own way.

At the beginning of the play two rituals, funeral and marriage, establish the tone and direction for Hamlet's rebellion. Both attempt to contain death and sexuality.[12] Hamlet will not accept these rituals and thus places himself on the edge of the action. Envision him as wearing a black sweat suit to the ritual occasion. He hasn't taken a bath for a month. During the course of the play, he draws entirely away from everyone except Horatio, who is a stranger at Elsinore, not really part of Danish society. Hamlet's drifting about on the periphery of his society is a ghostly action, like that of Old Hamlet, who's even now clumping around on the battlements and scaring the guards. Even as the play begins, we see young Hamlet locked into the dilemma that traps him throughout the play—he's saying to himself, "If I have to choose between madness and meaninglessness, I'll take madness, or what passes for it in this world of knaves and nitwits, where someone like Claudius is thought a reasonable man."

Look at Claudius's first words in the second scene of Act II, and notice what a fine fellow he is. He acknowledges his brother's death and everyone's grief, but says reason prevents him from tearing his hair out, like other people we could mention. He speaks in equivocal rhetorical figures, one word negating the other: "defeated joy, mirth in funeral, dirge in marriage." It's a verbal game well known to politicians. Claudius comes off as temperate, modest, reasonable. He warns the merrymakers of imminent war, appealing for unity against the enemy—the usual state of the union message, self-serving and pompous. Hamlet isn't buying it. He's still standing in the corner, silent, drawing the audience's eyes and interest to himself. Score one for Hamlet. The king disposes of state affairs, then switches gears and is an indulgent father to Laertes. He is ignoring Hamlet, who from the start is displaced as a son. Even if Hamlet wanted to join the world of this new father, he couldn't. Claudius has made it quite clear what kind of son he will accept—a young Rambo-in-training, dumb enough to be led by a villain. I don't care if you do Paris, Laertes, but check it out first with your dad, Claudius says. To be part of the world of the fathers in this play is to accept hierarchy, see lust as normal, and reject sensitivity as dangerous. Polonius, Laertes, and Claudius are cut from the same cloth. Only after he's disposed of all the court business does Claudius swing his swivel chair around like a corporate executive and go for Hamlet, saying: okay sonny, you're at the top of the food chain now, and you're about to be dead meat. Having dispatched the pressing affairs of state, Claudius is now ready to knock off details, of which Hamlet is one.

The king's tone is abrupt and hard, not indulgent as with Laertes. Hamlet, who knows it is unsafe to be direct, speaks in cautious metaphor. Elizabethans, of course, took their metaphors literally, and Hamlet means Claudius to. He says he's not in the dark but too much in the sun, meaning in the sunlight of masculine consciousness and reason. Gertrude nods in with words about the night, the dust of death, being a spokesperson for the grave. In Shakespeare, woman can archetypally be both grave and marriage bed, emblem of rotting and of birth. Hamlet, using metatalk, goes after her a bit more confidently than he did after Claudius, though he uses *double entendre*, to stay clear of the law. He tells her it's "common to die," meaning whorish to engage in sex, meaning Claudius and you are criminal degenerates. He uses words that are keys to the meaning of the play as a whole: Never mind seems, madam, it is. I'm not putting on a show for you, like some I could name. But what I feel is far beyond what I'm showing. The mystery of grief is past words or outward show. I'm in my transpersonal black suit, so leave me alone.

Claudius cuts in and attacks Hamlet rhetorically, saying that he's obstinate, impious, and, as a final *riposte*, that he is not a man. The real fight between them, throughout the play, is the denial of Hamlet's masculine identity and worth, his ability to play the manly role, or to wear the phallus, as Lacan would have it. Claudius twists the knife when he says Hamlet affronts reason "whose common theme is death of fathers" and which accepts loss and transition without unmanly, irrational grief. It's an unkind cut, since Hamlet, the philosophy student, prides himself most on his reason. If you want to join the world of the fathers, Claudius is saying to Hamlet, shut up and do what I tell you. Why? Because I'm the daddy, that's why.

Hamlet has a few choices at this point. He could be like Laertes and Fortinbras, shoving his bare bodkin down Claudius's traitorous throat and boldly claim the throne, or he could go back to grad school at Wittenberg and get his Ph.D., or he could do what mother wants and stepfather indulgently agrees to, because he thinks Hamlet's a wimp: he could stay on at court. What does he say? "I shall in all my best obey you, madam" (I,ii,126). He uses almost the same words Ophelia simpers to Polonius when he tells her to dump Hamlet. The whole court retires, leaving Hamlet to his ignominy as mother's boy, whipped to his knees by his surrogate father, and Hamlet bursts with all the tough talk he dared not spit out before.

He sees the state as metaphorically a garden full of stinkweed. His mother has married a goat-man, having forgotten the sun god his father, on whom she used to hang as if she could never get enough sex, a hint that Hamlet had been watching her for signs of concupiscence even before his father died. "Frailty, thy name is woman." Gertrude's no better than "a beast that wants discourse of reason," "posting with wicked speed to incestuous sheets." Hear the hissing, the hatred, the anger. At this point T. S. Eliot argues that Gertrude's sensuality is too small a cause for Hamlet's rage, misreading the entire play.

The real issue that male critics like Eliot, Jones, and even Lacan have avoided is Hamlet's failure to see and acknowledge the repression of his own femininity.[13] And what does femininity represent, in this context? It is the symbol of inner space, creativity, intuition, vulnerability, mystery. Erich Neumann writes of the creative man:

> Like the hero of myth, he stands in conflict with the world of the fathers, i.e., the dominant values, because in him the archetypal world and the self that directs it are such overpowering, living, direct experiences that they cannot be repressed. . . In the creative man . . . with his predominant mother archetype, the uncertain, wavering ego must itself take the exemplary, archetypal way of the hero; must slay the father.[14]

Such femininity is what Hamlet rejects, as he rejects Ophelia and his mother, thus rejecting his subjectivity, his emotions, his capacity for pain and love. He controls himself and others with words, words, words. Gertrude tells him in her bedroom that he uses them like a sword to cut her in two. Eliot reduces the focus of the play to Gertrude's failings, and then complains of the play's trivial cause. Jung would instead see the action in mythical terms: a conflict between the repressed mother/anima and the growing idea of the warrior father, burdened with his ideology of violence, power, revenge. The conflict goes on in the psyche of the hero as well as in the external world. Hamlet would be in agony even if Gertrude had killed herself in her filthy marriage bed. Had Gertrude not been available as a scapegoat, her son would have had to look at the real source of the problem—his own bond to the gentle, non-confrontational world of the mothers. Even when he chooses a male friend, he chooses a sweet, motherly one. It's no accident that Horatio appears precisely when Hamlet has just lost Gertrude and is about to lose Ophelia.

And where is Horatio, Hamlet's rational alter ego, while Hamlet's locked in verbal combat with Claudius? He's ghost-busting on the ramparts, determined to demonstrate rationally that nothing otherworldly exists in his rationalistic philosophy. In this scene, the first of Act I, we get a reading on the state of affairs in Denmark, seen from a perspective larger than Hamlet's. It is the last time we view the big picture. For the rest of the play, we see only Hamlet's side. Even when he kills Polonius and jokes about it, we're rooting for him. In *Othello* and *Macbeth*, Shakespeare gives us a rod by which to measure the hero's flaws, but not in *Hamlet*, which may be why Freud felt that Hamlet was Shakespeare himself.

Insight into Hamlet's state of mind, then, is not communicated by an omniscient Hamlet, as by a Prospero, but must be drawn from weaknesses he betrays rather than admits. Does he trust rather than mistrust, does he take initiative or feel guilt? Can he experience intimacy while preserving independence? Can he take on his parents as equals, or must he operate with them from a defensive position? On any recognized scale of psychological maturity, Hamlet at this point in the play would be a loser. He can manipulate but not control; he can curse but not cure; he can desire, but not love. At this point it seems like Hamlet is striking out every time. Still, we are on his side.

One reason we support Hamlet's view of the action is that we've seen the Ghost even before he has and know there's a tangle of mystery about the death of his father. Good men are sick at heart; Denmark is in darkness. One sentinel offers the other a basic metaphor for the whole play: "Stand and unfold yourself." Be seen, not seeming. Horatio initially thinks ghosts are only fantasies. In this matter of spirits, he's on the side of reason, like Claudius. Dead men stay dead. Seeing the Ghost harrows this rationalist with fear and wonder. Still, he challenges it, taking charge like a top sergeant. The Ghost walks away, insulted; Horatio pales and trembles. Reason has failed, not for the last time in the play. The reasonable, controllable world of the fathers is not to be trusted.

Shakespeare starts the play with a Ghost who represents another world, the old medieval world of the warrior, of the fathers before they were corrupted by lust and luxury. This world comes crashing in on that of the sons—boys, members of the Dead Poets' Society, students of philosophy, indulgers in the *dolce vita*, and makers of clever, shallow remarks. The private life, that of the child and the mother, is always under threat from the public, social life of the fathers, moving on the grand world stage with power and might, like the militant father God of Hebrews and Christians steamrolling the personal order of Jesus and Mary. Mythically, the real conflict going on in the play is between the personal world in which a man can risk loving and the public world where he must annihilate himself in service to the warrior ethic.

Hamlet moves from the light of Horatio's reason to the dark of the Ghost's passion easily, because he is moving within his own psyche. The Ghost is the symbol of the transpersonal beyond; he is the archetype of power, father, and paradoxically victim. The Ghost is a variation on the old vegetation myths where Isis buries her faceless son-lover-husband in the dark earth. He is a primitive Christ whose death shrinks the visible, pale, ordinary universe to nothing. Dominating the ego, the eye of reason, the light of day, he appears only as night terror in mystery and primeval chaos, where ego has no control. In the presence of the Ghost, the ego collapses, the unconscious erupts, and depersonalization occurs. Though Jung associates such terrors with the unconscious world of the mothers, in *Hamlet*, Gertrude causes no such irrational fits. She speaks for common sense, seeing no ghosts. So, paradoxically, in the beginning of the play, it is a male that lets us into the unconscious, the life beyond life, the magical, dark world of Hecate, the mythical goddess of death, darkness, retribution.

Ambivalence is Shakespeare's strong suit, as it is Hamlet's. Initially, the son regards the world of the father as dark, hellish, and an enemy. He will quickly come to see the father's world as heaven and the mother's as hell. The Ghost represents an unconscious psychic process pushing its way into consciousness. Jung believes the hero is likely to fail if he cannot integrate these two processes. Yet the first sign that the individual is about to be transformed is the awareness of some reality beyond the senses. Sensible Gertrude lives and dies unchanged, while Horatio begins as a skeptic and ends by praying for flights of angels to sing his sweet prince to rest. From Act I on, the contents of the unconscious are erupting like the Pacific Rim, and God help whoever's in the way. A child said, when asked if the ghost of Hamlet's father were really his father or the devil, "It's just the same. I think whoever tells you to kill someone *is* the devil." In one sense, the child was right. Hamlet is being invited to grow up and do his duty by the warrior standards of his day. His resistance to the Ghost's initiation is characteristic of what Jung called adolescent behavior, "a more or less patent clinging to the childhood level of consciousness, a resistance to the fateful forces in and around us which would involve us in the world" (*CW* 8,393/764). We see Hamlet between metaphor and metonymy, father and mother, coming apart at the seams.

The Ghost is real, in the world of the play. We cannot question the Ghost as Gertrude does, because we see it with our own eyes. The Ghost is both objectively real and subjectively a projection of something inside Hamlet. When Hamlet thinks of his mother, of women, he remembers the Ghost, acts like the Ghost, and talks like him, being cruel, implacable, and bent on revenge. Jung writes that the effect of such a transpersonal projection is "to isolate the subject from his environment, since instead of a real relation to it there is now only an illusory one. Projections change the world into the replica of one's unknown face" (*CW* 9ii, 9/17). And so it happens that the Ghost, Hamlet's projection of his own fear and desire, appears not just outwardly, but "in his mind's eye" (I,ii,195).

The Ghost's effect, whether good or evil, is also in the beholder's eye, for "there is nothing good or bad but thinking makes it so." Hamlet is already playing with renaissance relativism, having left the mother's world of mere being for the fine, brittle, abstract talk at Wittenberg. Translating the idea to act is not what he's especially good at. But he is not a bloodless philosopher, caught in the web of reason, as many critics have claimed; he's more of a poet, sniffing the cocaine of metaphor, paralyzed by poetry. If he can't act, it's not because he thinks too much, but because he feels too much, at least for himself and his own suffering. Coleridge sees Hamlet's problem as imbalance between inner and outer, being and doing. It's not what you've done that's important, Coleridge says in his *Notes on the Tragedies,* but what you are. The militant Ghost would not agree. His role is to initiate Hamlet into a harsh, achieving masculine world in which the erotic values of the mother have no place.

Ophelia's sentimental, girlish pain at his change means nothing to Hamlet. She reminds Hamlet of the old, childish days when they played in New Age workshops, feeling and sharing, dominated by women. Denmark was different then. The old father was still alive, and Hamlet could be a child. Now that the father is dead, he must leave childish things behind and become a father himself. Ophelia belongs to the fathers now and beckons Hamlet into their world, where he might become a father himself. To be a husband and father is either to be killed like old Hamlet or to be a killer like Claudius. To be a father means risking sex with a Gertrude.

Yet Ophelia and Hamlet play out the same scenario. Ophelia gets the word from her father and obeys it. She doubts the faith of her lover, baiting a trap to catch an offender against the father's law. She is shocked into madness by the murder of her father and lets herself drown, just as Hamlet feigns madness and is shipped off across the channel. Ophelia is Hamlet's mirror, his opposite number. Neither of them makes it into maturation. Neither communicates with the other. Othello and Desdemona move into the next stage of maturation: male taking on female as equal. But for Ophelia and Hamlet, there is only an embrace in the grave.

Hamlet tells Ophelia to immure herself in a nunnery and she accommodates him, going voluntarily to her death, the only suicide in a play rife with death wishes. For Hamlet, as for Jung's mythical heroes, the marriage bed is a grave of sorts, an extinction of the ego. Othello murdered his bride with his own hands. Hamlet drove his intended bride to kill herself. He never knew her, never wanted to, having his own fish to fry. Hamlet's erotic connection was not with Ophelia, but with Gertrude. In shielding Gertrude from Hamlet's jealous rage, the Ghost appealed to the warrior code: nature, blood, primitive revenge. He polarizes the masculine and the feminine. Rather than paddle fingers with Gertrude, old Hamlet had gone to war in Norway, avoiding Gertrude's seduction into the mother's anonymous erotic world. The mother is creative love and sensuality; the father is tough love and violence. Claudius represents both, a charming stinker, a sharp politician and womanizer. Unlike Hamlet, Claudius, on however low a level, has effected a Jungian integration of masculine and feminine. We may not like the way he did it, but he got the job done.

The Ghost tells Hamlet to be gentle with his guilty mother, suggesting a marginal acceptance of the feminine. Accepting his own feminine side, however, is the last thing Hamlet intends to do. Instead, he swears to wipe away all personal, "trivial, fond records." He will repress humanity, compromise, and gentleness in favor of blood revenge. When his friends come like Job's to sympathize with him, Hamlet talks to them as if through a megaphone, swearing them to silence. The Ghost gives us a menacingly vengeful voiceover. He's got Hamlet by the codpiece. It's the world of the fathers all the way from now on.

Right away, at the beginning of Act II an irregular pulse in the play occurs. The action is uncertain, multiple plots spin off, nobody knows what's going on, except maybe the Ghost, popping in from Purgatory every so often. Instead of the single-minded, hurtling drive forward apparent in *Macbeth* and *Othello*, the structure of *Hamlet* is erratic like Hamlet himself–like life, or dream. The hero's internal conflict between maternal and paternal values shadows the whole play as it shadows his own maturation.

From the beginning of the play, Hamlet has a foot in each world. The beginning of Act II offers a glimpse of the real, daylight world, where mediocre, self-serving ordinary men are going about business as usual. Polonius sends out spies on his son Laertes, playboy in Paris, telling them "by indirections find directions out," a description of *Hamlet's* whole structure. Earlier, Polonius gave his son advice, much as the Ghost gave advice to Hamlet. Both these old fathers try to teach their sons to negotiate the world like a minefield, to learn young how to play the game, fight dirty, and win. The fathers create divisions between their sons and everybody else, initiating the young men into a world of separation, manipulation, self-protection, and pulling them by the forceps of reason, law, and self-interest, out of the womb of feckless boyhood. The boys are being conditioned to be tough, controllers of the situation, builders of a working persona. They are being taught to go to war with the world in order to survive as efficient egos. Kill or be killed. That's the word from the fathers. Claudius was the only one who received the message, until he made a fatal mistake: loving Gertrude so much that he did not have Hamlet skewered in an alley before the end of Act I.

In Act III, Claudius is wearing his persona of the good, concerned king and stepfather, manipulating Hamlet's school friends, Rosencrantz and Gildenstern, as self-serving a pair of hustlers as ever got theirs. Claudius nudges them with an elbow in the ribs and a leer, saying they should lure Hamlet into "pleasures," while Gertrude offers them a bribe if they can figure out what's bothering her son. These two spies are like Tweedledum and Tweedledee: obedient, no questions asked, no individuation, no conscience. Just bodies doing a job and deserving exactly what they get, as does Claudius, who has set these craven, inconsequential dogs on his stepson.

Claudius, in his later soliloquy, says it hurts him to look at the murder of his brother and compares himself to a whore. His tragedy is precisely his self-knowledge, in which he is one step ahead of Hamlet. He knows his crime, but cannot admit it publicly or give up its fruits. He is too stuck in his desire for Gertrude. Claudius is not the self-serving monster in *Hamlet* that he is in Shakespeare's sources. We know his human side from his brief soliloquies. At this point, before the letter scene with Ophelia, he thinks Hamlet may be like himself, an ordinary, lovesick fellow. If we can just get the boy married off, send the honeymoon couple to Paris, and keep Gertrude happy, Claudius thinks, all may yet be well. He doesn't know who Hamlet is, thinks he's a young wimp, and has the businessman's contempt for scholars and poets. By the end of Act III, scene one, he'll have smartened up. But just now, he's hoping for the best. He is clearly an example of what the medieval renaissance psychologists called a sanguine type. Claudius is bloody, hot, moist, energetic, and hopeful—a Jack Kennedy, while Hamlet is melancholic, full of black bile, gloomy, apprehensive, and solitary. The humors flow from prolonged moral crisis and a lack of moderation which brings on a lack of harmony. An excess of passion leads to ill health of mind and body. Most of us are dominated by one humor, and Hamlet's was black melancholia. The two father figures hiding behind the curtain watching him and Ophelia were not far off the mark when they feared Hamlet was sliding into the world of the maternal eros, into subjectivity, madness, and love.

Another vision of the real, political world and its obedient servants is shown to Hamlet and the audience by Polonius and Ophelia. She is set up by the king and her father to manipulate and trick Hamlet, whose poor little love poems, the awkward fantasies of an adolescent lover, are read by the cold eyes of the court. "In her excellent white bosom, etc.," he writes, clumsy at romantic manipulation. Polonius clucks disapproval at Hamlet's diction—"the beautified Ophelia" he notes, "Vile phrase, vile phrase." We're getting a heavy dose of the real, ugly world which Hamlet is reluctant to enter. No wonder we sympathize with Hamlet and the dream world of the son, lover, student—he's an innocent alien, chased around the stage by scientists intent on vivisection. Hamlet was not part of Claudius's Machiavellian renaissance world. Machiavelli said in *The Prince*, "There is such a distance between how men do live and how men ought to live, that he who leaves that which is done for that which ought to be done learns sooner his ruin than his preservation."

Machiavelli is talking about the man who can't tell the ideal world from the real one. He is talking about men like Hamlet.

Jung might say that the myth Hamlet lives out is that of the innocent child Galahad, victimized by shrewd, callous adults, courtiers mocking his childish sweetness, though in the end he finds the Holy Grail and shows up all the cynics. Hamlet meets his old friends openly, ready to love them as he loves the more worthy Horatio. Only when he sees they are false does his childlike trust vanish, does he see them as clanking machine-men sent by his stepfather to set him up. Hamlet probes, having learned some of the world's tricks by now: "Were you not sent for?" He is desperate, wanting them to stand and unfold themselves, free of mere seeming: "Come, come! Nay, speak!" You can see them glancing at each other, shuffling, looking down at their feet, anywhere but into Hamlet's disappointed eyes. Suddenly the curtain falls between them and the prince. Hamlet grows cold, mocking them for their nervous, conciliatory giggling, breaking once and for all the boyhood bond that linked them. Later, he has them murdered, "hoist by their own petard," as carelessly as he will kill Polonius, lugging the guts into the neighbor room. Dead, for a ducat, dead.

But in Act II, Polonius is still alive and plotting. "I plot therefore I am," is the motto of Polonius, a real Machiavellian. He tries to prove Hamlet is mad for love of Ophelia and is not put off by being called a fishmonger. Even dull, smug Polonius realizes Hamlet is tweaking his beard. If the prince is mad, his madness has some method in it, like the structure of the whole drama. Even Polonius is dimly aware that his idea of the world is only a holding action against chaos and old night, against a reality larger, deeper, and more terrifying than his poor pea-brain can handle. All the advice of Polonius to Laertes, Ophelia, and to the rulers is perfectly sensible, if you discount the world outside his cramped little closet of reason and worldly craft. Shakespeare puts all the clichés of sensible, conservative politicians in the mouth of Polonius, "To thine own self be true...It is common for the younger sort to lack discretion," but all the while he is craftily and by indirection trying to get a prince for a son-in-law, a hustle which would make Polonius ultimately into a king's father-in-law. Though he speaks self-deprecatingly, saying to Gertrude and Claudius that Ophelia has no right to look so high for a husband, he knows better. Later, when Ophelia is dead, Gertrude says she had hoped to lay flowers on the marriage bed of Ophelia and Hamlet. So, this marriage was not impossible. Polonius is just acting, "seeming," playing his hand cautiously, like any good businessman.

Hamlet strolls on the scene of Polonius's making, probably aware of the old father-counselor's manipulation, and meets Ophelia, who's been set up and is having trouble handling her lines. Hamlet cannot have missed seeing Polonius scurry behind the curtain, already bulging with Claudius, who, as a plump, sanguine type, is causing the curtain to bulge quite a bit. At first, Hamlet gives Ophelia a chance to be honest, though he's angry at having his gifts and poems returned. Poets tend to be touchy about such matters. She might have signalled him that they were being watched, or have passed him a note, but no, she was a good renaissance daughter, daddy's girl. Ophelia is playing the game of the sweet young thing; she doesn't know any other game to play. Hamlet tells her to go to a nunnery, where she won't be a breeder of sinners like Gertrude, Claudius, and himself. Turning on the very idea of generation, of bearing children and the future, Hamlet admits to being a monster. Down with the world of the mothers, he says. Down with having children. We suddenly see Hamlet as he sees himself—not a Hyperion like his perfect father, but an ineffective, arrant knave.

Despite his cruelty, we do not stop loving him. His dramatic rhetoric is hyperbolic and ironic. Every word he says must be seen in the context of every other word. He offers riddles, doesn't let his questioners finish their speeches, upsets their prejudices, literalizes their metaphors, metaphorizes their literal remarks. He equivocates, meaning that his own fluid, paradoxical view of the world collides with the rigid, traditional model of those around him. He ridicules the *status quo* with a new, self-created language, his only form of power. He substitutes new linguistic structures for the old, rigid, false ones, which is why new literary critics like Derrida and Serpieri are looking less at general structure in Shakespeare, or paradigmatics, and more at syntagmatics, that is, the syntactic level of dramatic discourse. When Claudius properly scolds Hamlet, "Now where's Polonius," a question that assumes his kingly, fatherly authority and ignores the fact that Polonius is actually dead, Hamlet answers from the world of irony, paradox, and sensory experience: "You shall nose him as you go up the stairs." Here we have an example of "spoken action," an interchange not only of characters, but of two different ideological and verbal models—two languages clashing dramatically.[15]

Trouble is, Hamlet's too verbal for his own good. He is busily digging his own grave in this confrontational scene with Ophelia, and even more in the mousetrap play-within-a-play that's coming up. Over the crumpled, crying heap of Ophelia, he shouts in the direction of the bulging curtain: "Those that are married already—all but one—shall live."

Nothing like telling everything you know to get you into trouble. This Claudius is no dummy. When Hamlet's run off the stage, the king comes storming back on, shouting: the hell you say Hamlet's crazy. He's out to kill somebody, probably me. I'll pack him off to my buddy, the king of England, who will blow him away as a favor to his fellow king. In England, no one, especially Gertrude, will lay the crime to him. Claudius leaves us in no doubt that it's all-out war from now on, and Hamlet, knowing nothing of his uncle's intentions, is unarmed. While Claudius schemes, Hamlet is sinking in the swampy mother-world of feelings.

Hamlet is helpless because he has failed to acknowledge his ambivalent reaction to the perfect man—his Ghost-Father. Young Hamlet cannot end his grieving because the ambivalence hasn't surfaced in his consciousness. More important for the structure of the play, his inability to kill Claudius has a Freudian connection to his ambivalence about his own father. Unconsciously, Hamlet enjoys the incestuous activities of the man he hates and doesn't want them to stop. He is projecting his own mother-love onto Claudius and sabotaging his Ghost-Father's command for revenge. The failure of Hamlet's only aggressive action, the Dumb-show, offers evidence of the prince's double-mindedness.

Just after Rosencrantz and Guildenstern have shown themselves as they really are, Hamlet reconnects with the actors, his old friends. He is no longer an innocent but wants to use them to check out the Ghost's story. He orders them to act out an episode from the Trojan War, a war over a woman. The Bronze Age warriors of Greece conquered the old mother-goddess cultures of Anatolia or Troy. Shakespeare unknowingly created a perfect symbol of this conquest in Hamlet's Dumb-show. The destruction of the great parent city of the civilized late Neolithic world by the new warrior culture from the north, this matricide of nations, was a triumph of the fathers.

Yet all is not well in this triumph over the mother's city that sheltered Helen and was ruled by Hecuba. When "the unnerved father falls," Pyrrhus, son of dead Achilles, goes after Priam, the king of Troy and father figure/king par excellence. When Pyrrhus has King Priam at his feet, "Pyrrhus stood/and like a neutral to his will and matter, *did nothing*"(II,ii,453). Later, of course, Pyrrhus does Priam in, but the words "did nothing" ring in our ears. They foreshadow the battle Hamlet will have within himself between hesitation and action, thought and deed, his mother-self and his father-self. And Hamlet's tears over Hecuba, the Great Mother of fallen Troy, are more than tears for a dead heroine of myth—they are tears for the dead feminine within himself, lost with the betrayals of Gertrude and Ophelia, who ally themselves with Claudius, the intruder-father, the false father, unknowingly build-ing a wall between Hamlet and his woman-side. Their task is to unite with the male power, his is to kill its possessor and seize power himself. The king must die, long live the king: an old myth from the Neolithic village days.

A hero who cannot perceive or integrate the psychic processes surfacing in his consciousness will not achieve individuation, but will come to a tragic end.[16] When a hero in a position of power is obsessed by his anima, his private maternal eros and is unable to integrate his public, paternal logos, he finds himself unable to act effectively in the real world of power plays and politics. "The persona, the ideal picture of a man as he should be, is inwardly compensated by feminine weakness, and as the individual outwardly plays the strong man," as Hamlet does in this act and the next, "so he becomes inwardly a woman, i.e., the anima" (*CW* 7,194/309). So paradoxically the tougher and more manly Hamlet's persona gets, the more anima-ridden, manic, and unreasonable his unconscious becomes. He screams at Laertes over Ophelia's grave, then calmly apologizes, saying he wasn't himself. As Hamlet puts on and takes off masks, his maturation process aborts. The contents of the unconscious are polarized, not assimilated. Other heroes join with their anima or their shadow: by the time Macbeth dies, he becomes a feelingless zombie; he becomes his own shadow, that piece of himself represented by the vicious witch, Lady Macbeth, while Othello becomes his shadow Iago, who exists only as a sort of bitch-travesty of his own anima and hated wife, Emilia. Hamlet ends by becoming a death machine, cold and fatalistic. He never gets as far as marriage, which Macbeth and Othello do, never begins peace talks with his mother or his lover—they are forever the enemy. He hates himself, wants to die, wants to join his father. If he can't stand shoulder to shoulder with Old Hamlet in violence, he'll consider suicide as a serious option.

Between Jung's "extremes of self-knowledge and negation of self," Hamlet flounders like the poor Father-Ghost, between heaven and hell, day and night, forever doomed to dissolve at dawn. Hamlet the son has felt the awareness of a reality "beyond the range of visual experience. . .the first step in the transformation of the individual from fragmentary ego-consciousness to a realization of the self." If the ego succeeds in assimilating the contents of the unconscious, the ideal of completeness becomes an attainable aim. For the self "is an ever-present archetype of wholeness which may easily disappear from the purview of consciousness" (*CW* 9ii,13/14). Because other people sense that Hamlet cares nothing for the world and the people around him, they are afraid. The stink of the Ghost, of death, is on Hamlet, and he's depressing to have around. He feels the same way about himself, and we see him quick to hate, blame, and kill because he sees not Self when he looks inward, but Mother—her frailty, her lust, her fear. If he could find his father inside himself, he would not need to seek him on the battlements, and he would not doubt his father's word about Claudius. He would cut his uncle down without a qualm. But Claudius is a projection of himself as he would like to be—king, father, lover to Gertrude the Great Mother, her Twin Soul. To kill Claudius, his shadow, is to kill himself, and so it turns out in Act V, when the two die together, at opposite ends of a sword.

The tragedy of Hamlet is that he failed to integrate the contents of his unconscious, failed to make conscious the faceless demons that rode him in the dark, failed to reach individuation. His ego is defeated or "swallowed" in Jung's words, by his mother, his subjective side, of whom he was so afraid that he would rather die than accept her common, earthy sensuality. When he decides to become a warrior, he buries his feminine nature alive, and is therefore ineffective, almost to the end. Because Hamlet cannot integrate intuition and action, he, like the Ghost, is forced to walk only in medial dawn, neither here nor there. Things happen to him; he does not make them happen.

The pathos of his situation is that he is a renaissance man, living in a relativistic, modern, Montaignian world of shifting values. Not the sublime certitude and glory of platonic idealism, but randomness, flux, and meaninglessness are at the heart of the new renaissance rationalism. Shakespeare, man of intuition and mystery that he was, knew that such a world divorced from the feminine, from the heart, could end only in a bath of blood, whether at Elsinore, revolutionary Paris, or Tiananmen Square. Eliot said of the Elizabethan Age that it was the last in the west to experience the unity of thought and feeling. That linkage is what metaphor is all about, combining the two as when chaotic Denmark becomes "unweeded garden." Hamlet's dilemma was an acting out of the modern breakdown that was to come between the head and the heart, the conscious mind and the unconscious. Throughout the play, Hamlet is poised to act, but cannot, for he knows that action will commit him irrevocably to the world of the fathers, in which his artist's soul will die in unwilling combat. He can't go back into the world of the mothers for it would swallow him and his budding ego alive. The father's world is all he has, and his thoughts are "bloody or nothing worth."

In taking up what Erikson calls his "negative identity," Hamlet becomes "exactly what his own ethical sense could not tolerate: a mad revenger."[17] He embraces the archetype of the warrior, the very opposite of the maternal eros. Not until after his capture by pirates, the first test of his manhood outside his family world, does Hamlet begin the conjunction of opposites which Jung believed was necessary to maturation:

> If the ego does not interfere with its irritating rationality, the opposites, just *because* they are in conflict, will gradually draw together, and what looked like death and destruction will settle down into a latent state of concord, suitably expressed by the symbol of pregnancy. (*CW* 14,360/ 506)

Hamlet's ego interrupts the conjunction of the opposites until almost the end of the play. He dies pregnant with a stillborn Self.

Until events propelled Hamlet into the warrior's world, he was living the archetype of the eternal boy (*puer aeternus*), "narcissistic, inspired, effeminate, phallic, inquisitive, inventive, passive, fiery, and capricious." [18] Many archetypes merge in him, but the dominant characteristic of them all is a "special relation with the transcendent spiritual powers of the collective unconscious."[19] The *puer* whose "transcendent call" is heard from within an entangling family web tries to become the family messiah, like Hamlet, instead of realizing the mature Self and leaving the family behind for the world at large. Like the ancient Thracian Dionysius-Zagreus, who changed from beautiful youth to raging bull, Hamlet projects by turns his sweetness and his fury at both parents. Such anger assists emotional separation from the parents and begins the initiation into manhood. During the initiatory period, the *puer* lives in self-centered isolation, behaving outrageously and experimentally. He may cause distress to those who want to "keep the child cribbed," in order to stop his development.[20]

Hamlet's main experiment, his one effort to control the action is the mousetrap, play-within-a-play. Typical of him, the effort is theater—a work of art. "The play's the thing wherein I'll catch the conscience of the king." He means to catch the Ghost/King in a lie, if the Ghost is lying, or to convict King Claudius publicly of murder, if he is a murderer. But Hamlet's own perturbed spirit prevents him from doing either. Throughout the experiment, he is the uncommitted and playful *puer*.

What Hamlet hopes to get out of the mousetrap play is very much what Claudius wanted to get out of the play in which Ophelia returned Hamlet's gifts and poems. These two "mighty opposites" have certain qualities and actions in common. They both love Gertrude, produce plays intended to trick the other into self-revelation, and engage in bouts of self-hatred. As Claudius wants to flush out his nephew's intent, Hamlet wants to prove the Ghost right and to convict Claudius publicly of murder. Claudius was supposed to run sobbing from the room when the player-nephew poured poison in the player-king's ear, and as he ran, cry out that he was guilty of his brother's murder. Such a solution is typical of Hamlet. He thinks art and intellect can make a perfect world, one that is fair and honest. He wants his stepfather to admit his guilt, be savaged by the court, stripped of his kingship, convicted of murder, and executed. Very convenient. Hamlet could then congratulate himself on having carried out the Ghost's commands but without bloodying himself in his uncle's blood without committing himself to the world of the fathers, without earning the hatred of his mother, and above all, without killing his own shadow, that man who had done what Hamlet wished to do, possess Gertrude—or, if you read the play in Jungian terms, that man who had progressed in maturation far enough to love a woman, accept his subjectivity, his feelings, act on them, and still function effectively in the world of men. Hamlet could not, in fact, kill Claudius without killing off the very man he wished to become, would become if he grew up and someday became a king. So the Mouse-trap is the perfect intellectual's solution. All Hamlet has to do is to sit back, his head in Ophelia's lap, laughing it up, and watching Claudius give himself, the kingdom, and Gertrude away. Claudius does no such thing. Instead, Hamlet shoots himself in the foot.

Throughout the Mouse-trap exercise, Hamlet is manic, playing word-games with Claudius, who is grave and guarded. Hamlet remarks lightly that great men die and are forgotten and that he for one will enjoy life, for it's running out. Hamlet rattles on, his persona in place, pretending to be both mad and in love, not realizing that Claudius knows he's neither, that in fact he's long since tipped his hand to this crafty, worldly father-figure.

Hamlet gets more excited as the Dumb-show goes on. He says "the players cannot keep counsel. They'll tell all." Exactly what he's about to do. The players say the words he would tell the world, but not in his own voice: "Our thoughts are ours, their ends none of our own." These words, placed in the player's mouth remind us that Hamlet comes from the personal world and will never play on the public stage. He can create causes, spin off ideas, but he cannot control effects. He hangs like the Ghost between night and day, heaven and earth.

Just after the player-queen has vowed fidelity to her lord, Hamlet asks Gertrude how she likes the play. Gertrude says indifferently, "the lady doth protest too much." Gertrude isn't much for extremes and abstractions. She's a practical, earthy woman, who would never carry on like an opera about fidelity. She simply takes life and love as they come, not dealing in polarities as her son does. Clearly, she isn't upset, isn't guilty, and Hamlet turns his moral klieg light on Claudius, who up to now has been feeling Gertrude's thigh, drinking mead from his Rangers' mug, totally ignoring the show. He is probably plastered. Suddenly he straightens up and asks sharply, "What do you call this play, anyway?" Hamlet begins to talk too much, too fast, the curse of nervous intellectuals, wanting to tell all they know:

> This play is the image of a murder done in Vienna. Gonzago
> is the duke's name; his wife, Baptista. You shall see anon.
> 'Tis a knavish piece of work, but what of that? Your
> majesty, and we that have free souls, it touches us not. Let
> the galled jade wince, our withers are unwrung. This is one
> Lucianus, nephew to the king.

The play, he says gratuitously, is about the way a nephew murders his lord and marries his duchess. A few lines later, Hamlet irrepressibly pipes up again: "He poisons him in the garden for's estate. . . You shall see anon how the murderer gets the love of Gonzago's wife." Gonzago was the sleeping king who just had poison poured into his ears. At this point, Claudius yells for lights, takes off with the whole court, and Hamlet dances around the stage, pleased with himself. Horatio doesn't seem much impressed with Hamlet's performance, but speaks dryly, tersely: "You might have rhymed." That is, "you might have kept some order, some structure in what you said." It's the closest that sweet, motherly Horatio comes to criticism of his friend.

Too bad, for Hamlet needed to hear the truth. What had happened in this mousetrap, this aesthetic creation of Hamlet's that was to convict the king? It proved nothing. The king ran out of the room when Hamlet's play showed a nephew assassinating a king. The whole court, including Hamlet's mother is shocked and mad at him (III, ii, 78-302). A king has been threatened. Hamlet had not shut up and let the play do its work, had not given Claudius a chance to admit his crime publicly. Instead, Hamlet interrupted, babbled, gave away the farm. He has now proved to Claudius that keeping his young nephew around would be suicidal, and unlike Hamlet, Claudius is not into self-destruction.

Even when the aborted little play is over, and Tweedledum and Tweedledee, his one-time friends, arrive to tell him Claudius has not taken the mousetrap kindly, Hamlet is so manic he's jumping out of his skin. He toys with the Tweedles, saying he's in a bad mood because he wants to be king. They remind him he's been promised the throne after Claudius. Power is not what Hamlet is after. What he wants is to be his own man, not to be manipulated and kicked in the head anymore. He asks Guildenstern to play his recorder, but Guildenstern has no music. Hamlet then says, you can't play the pipe, but you try to play me, to "pluck out my mystery," to steal my privacy, my feelings. He has their number, and just in time, for the next thing we see is the king sending the Tweedles off to England with a secret letter to have Hamlet murdered.

About this time we get a last glimpse of Claudius alone. He has been drawn into more murder in order to save his skin. He wants to be forgiven by God but knows that to be forgiven, he must give up his power, admit his guilt, and lose both his throne and Gertrude. Claudius says he can't make a move without Gertrude, which means he's just as unable to kill Hamlet as Hamlet is to kill him. The mighty opposites are now locked in mortal combat.

Throughout the play we hear echoes of the mythical conflict between patriarchal and matriarchal systems where the old Hecate myths began. Hecate turns up more than once in this play. She is the goddess who represents the old polygamous cults in the Aegean, before the conquest by the monogamous patriarchs. Her poison, Hebenon, is poured in the king's ear. This mythical sister of Isis and Kali is invoked three times in the Dumb-show. Fertile and bloodthirsty, she is both witch and goddess, as Hamlet perceives Gertrude in the next scene. Hecate is associated with stabbing, poisoning, and the breaking up of relationships, as she is in *King Lear*. Hamlet explicitly sees Claudius as a disciple of Hecate, as he makes clear in the mousetrap. When Hamlet refers to his mother's bestial nature, he is referring to Hecate, who is represented by the lion, the dog, and the mare—all of them sexy, all of them powerful. Gertrude, as Hecate's stand-in, would draw Hamlet into unconsciousness, lust, and murder. She would draw him again into compromise with the world as it is. "The prayer to Hecate...is not necessarily even addressed to this or that goddess of the Greek myth, but to the speaker's own unconscious urge to identify himself with one of nature's archetypal emanations of darkness."[21] Hamlet's situation has been orchestrated by himself. He has no one else to blame, though he tries hard to find a scapegoat: first Ophelia, then Gertrude.

Now, to the famous scene in Gertrude's closet. Olivier and Nicolson played it mostly on her couch, and Gertrude's closet was where Jones found his Freudian inspiration. To gain ascendancy over his mother, Hamlet uses poetry, a mirror, his father's sanctity, and a guilt trip. Gertrude cries out that he's going to murder her, and so he is—in himself. He's going to stop being her mirror and substitute an actual one. They will both see the truth in the mirror. No more seeming. Gertrude rightly guesses this maneuver is a kind of death threat. Hamlet is killing the woman in himself, and, as is evident later, the results of his actions will kill his mother.

On the job as always, hiding behind Gertrude's curtain, Polonius yells for help, and Hamlet stabs him, hoping that by accident he's killed the king. When the prince learns that he has killed only his former love's father, he goes right back to pounding Gertrude into the ground of her guilt. Having determined that her crime is incest only, not murder, Hamlet tells her she has no right to be interested in sex at her age, pandering her reason to her will/desire. Her only crime is that she enjoys sex with her husband. Hamlet reproaches her for her sensuality until even the implacable Ghost-Father drifts in to remind him that his duty is not to make women cry, but to kill a murderer. Hamlet's having a fine time, his diatribe against female sexuality in full swing, but is cut short. After his father's appearance, he tells his mother to stop letting Claudius call her his mouse and paddle her neck with his damned fingers. Refrain from sex one night at a time, he suggests, like an AA member from drink. He wants her to promise him to go to a convent and stay away from those paddling fingers, but all Gertrude promises is not to report on him to Claudius. Clearly, Hamlet can no longer rely on her. Whether or not he wants the split from the maternal eros, it's happened.

Claudius, needing no advice from Gertrude, has already sent a request to the English king to wipe out Hamlet in a fraternal act of solidarity. When Claudius tells Hamlet in Act IV, scene iii to go to England, Hamlet looks him in the eye and knows Claudius's purpose is murder. Strangely, he calls Claudius his "dear mother." Why? Because Claudius is taking him to his death, and the mother is the mythical figure for ego-death in Shakespeare as in Jung. She is the grave, the body, the ego-annihilating earth. Claudius, for his part, feels Hamlet as he feels Gertrude—"like a hectic in the blood." As is Hamlet, Claudius is being pushed to the wall. Neither has any more options. They could not kill the other when the time was right, and now they will go down together, in a mortal embrace that is as much love as hate. Gertrude will be crushed between these mighty opposites, for it is love of her that joins them like shadows to their source.

Before he leaves Denmark, Hamlet has a brief brush with Fortinbras, his replacement. Fortinbras is a forthright, simple fellow, who does his duty without a thought of guilt. Fortinbras is the litmus paper by which Hamlet must test his resolve. The Norwegian is the son who has grown up to become a father, a warrior, as Hamlet never will. At the thought of him, Hamlet feels a rush of self-hatred and ends the scene by saying, "O, from this time forth, my thoughts be bloody, or be nothing worth." Fortinbras has whipped Hamlet into a fine lather, and the Danish prince takes off across the sea, away from his mother, to test himself in a man's world. Hamlet increasingly tries to be in his father's mode, even carrying his signet and the dueling sword. When he finally stabs Claudius, he is, for a moment, king, one last identity tried on before death: "Identity can only be an experimental truth. It is confirmed in the moment of challenge, of action."[22]

Meanwhile, Ophelia has gone mad at the loss of her father, a madness which Hamlet only pretended. On her babbling surface float the repressed contents of her childish mind—sensuality, and doubt of her identity (IV,v,45). Claudius, bless his sentimental heart, is touched and wants her taken care of. Horatio is given the job, but fails at it owing to his concern for Hamlet. Like most murderers, Claudius has the virtue of his defects: maudlin pity for others and himself (IV,ii,13-45). He is terrified that the murder of Polonius will unseat him from his throne and thinks of nothing but protecting himself, just as Hamlet thinks of little but destroying himself. One is the photographic negative of the other. Laertes has come storming back, ready to kill, ready to become king, and says to Claudius what Hamlet wanted to say but never could: "Oh thou vile king/Give me my father" (IV,v,12-13). Claudius treats him man-to-man: Be calm, he says, for "such a divinity doth hedge a king." Let me tell you who killed your father and help you avenge yourself. He echoes Hamlet's diction in the line, "such a divinity doth shape our ends" (V,ii,10). The two are polarizing as the climax of the play approaches.

The conspiracy against Hamlet has begun. Claudius has a new son, Laertes, and his son will do for the father, for Polonius, what Hamlet could not do for his murdered king. While the two of them plot, mad Ophelia throws flowers and wild words around the room, undermining their reason with the dark, allusive language of the unconscious. Laertes weeps for Ophelia, but forces himself not to let out his tears, the woman in him. Instead, he chooses the man's part, justice and murder.

Hamlet has been eluding death during Act IV, floating on the dangerous sea of the unconscious, evading pirates. Unlike Ophelia, he does not drown, though that part of him sinks which was innocent, which loved, felt, and suffered. When Hamlet declaims over her dead body, after his musings on the death of Yorick the jester, he grieves over his own as well. He's just been looking at Yorick's clacking jawbone, where once the lips hung that the child Hamlet kissed. Entropy, entropy, all is entropy. This renaissance commonplace takes on a literal meaning with Hamlet. He has begun to learn the lesson he would not learn earlier in his suicidal soliloquies. The ego has no place to go once it dies, and it will die, as even Alexander and Hamlet's father died. What Claudius told him in Act I about death's inevitability is finally sinking in. No fine words, private passions, or intellectual games will save him. Hamlet has become cold and fatalistic. It's as if he's suddenly grown a foot taller than all the others on the stage and sees over their heads into the next life, the place of ghosts and lost causes. "The cat will mew," he says, "and dog will have its day." Only the man's world is on the stage now. Hamlet's options are gone—it's kill and replace Claudius or die a victim of his own passivity.

Hamlet's persona in Act V, scene ii is now firmly in place. He laughs at the death of the Tweedles. His humor is fierce and bitter. When he talks of the English king (ll. 40-50), his rhetoric is as political and cool as that of Claudius. Killing the Tweedles is not on his conscience, for "they did make love to this employment." They asked for it. A man's life is brief anyway, he shrugs, "no more than to say one" (V,ii,57-58). Hamlet, after the cathartic blowup at Ophelia's grave, is like a man who's gone through primal scream therapy. He is calm, observant, detached, with no illusions about himself. If he can win the fight with Laertes, fine. If not, Claudius will lose his wager. Hamlet doesn't care whether he wins or loses, lives or dies. Here again we see him unwilling to make the step into autonomous manhood, just as he is unwilling to go back and sit in the lap of Gertrude or Ophelia. Events simply happen to him, and he takes control of nothing. He talks like a zombie; "the bubbles are out." He is polite but remote. To Horatio, who fears that Hamlet will lose this wager, Hamlet says he probably won't, however, "thou wouldst not think how ill all's here about my heart. But it is no matter." Again he's caught between emotion "that would trouble the heart of a woman" (V,ii,215) and tough, fatalistic cool. "The readiness is all. . .Let be." Hamlet returns to his classical training, echoing the Stoic philosophers and Horatio, saying that it is not the time of man's death but the manner of it that is important. He's entered the world of men, but he's almost lost his capacity for feeling in the process. In their civilized little speeches before the last fight, Hamlet and Laertes make clear that they are "doubles"—one that must fight, the other that is "satisfied." That is, they are both feminine and masculine, ready to do, ready to be. It's the closest Hamlet comes to balance in the play and hints at an initiation and rebirth that die aborning.

The two young men are not at the same stage of psychic development, however. Laertes already belongs to the masculine world and kills on cue. Hamlet does not. After the play, he considers killing Claudius at prayer. More significantly, Hamlet does not kill the king on his return from England, though he could prove to the world that Claudius had tried to kill him. Rather than bring back the incriminating letter conveyed by the Tweedles, he used it to kill the luckless students and returns to Denmark empty-handed. Not the wisest move. Hamlet no longer sees the Ghost, no longer seems intent on killing Claudius. Something has shifted in him since the return from the sea, the pirates, and near-death.

At the beginning of the duel in Act V, the Claudius side of Hamlet has not completely surfaced to Hamlet's consciousness, while his Gertrude side has fallen with Ophelia into the grave. Even Claudius says Laertes cannot hit Hamlet at this moment (V,ii,277). Laertes says the act is almost against his conscience—but Hamlet calls him on. Do "your best violence." To be or not to be, Hamlet says, almost gaily, come on, man, strike, you're making a wanton of me, meaning, you're playing with me as with a woman. He seems to be asking Laertes to kill him, even though Hamlet hasn't yet carried out his manly duty of killing Claudius. He has not yet joined the world of the fathers, which would complete his initiation.

But now Gertrude takes up the poisoned cup, drinks to Hamlet's health, and wipes his brow. In a single motion, she demonstrates her love of life and her motherly care for her son. Laertes wounds Hamlet with the poisoned foil point (Hecate speaks again from the world under appearances, from the unconscious), and Gertrude falls over, dying. "How does the Queen?" Hamlet says, stopping the movie. He's about to find out that the embodiment of all his fantasies, all his projections, is stone dead. Now mortality has to be faced.

Gertrude cries out that she's poisoned: "O my dear Hamlet, the drink. . ." She drinks Claudius's poison literally as she once did metaphorically. At this moment, Hamlet bellows like a bull full of picks. All his cool evaporates, and he's the avenger he never was for his father. "Let the door be locked. Treachery! seek it out." Laertes admits he was working with the king. "The king, the king's to blame," and all cry "Treason." Claudius is publicly convicted, at least of trying to kill his nephew, and Hamlet need not have lifted his sword again.

But something has changed. Hamlet finally acts, and except for Freudian Ernest Jones, critics have never pointed out precisely why. Yes, it's the end of Act V and time for the late bus home. But the something more is that Gertrude's been killed. Although Hamlet's been unable to attack Claudius for five solid acts, he stabs him with a poisoned sword three lines after Laertes tells him that Claudius's Tequila Sunrise has killed Gertrude. And Hamlet isn't content with the stab of a mere poisoned sword. He jumps onto the table, falls on Claudius like Batman, and forces the rest of the potion down his uncle's throat. "Is thy union here? [Thy onion, thy pearl, metaphorically, Claudius's soul.] Follow my mother."

As Othello will die in tandem with his shadow Iago after the murder of Desdemona, so Hamlet dies beside father/uncle Claudius, almost in the act of throttling him. Only when he and his structures have fallen apart does Hamlet begin to find a new identity. As Hillman says, "falling apart makes possible a new style of reflection within the psyche. Pathologizing is the royal road to soul-making." Miguel de Unamuno observes, "It is not upon life that our ultimate individuality centers, but upon death."[23] In the last moments before his death, talking to Horatio, Hamlet becomes the king, sorting out final arrangements for the kingdom, for his funeral, and for his reputation. We will see Othello doing the same thing. Neither of them lives to complete his integration, because neither acknowledges the woman in himself.

Hamlet's last thoughts are for his reputation and the state, not for his lost mother. Gertrude lies in the corner, her toes turned up, and he gives her not a glance, not a word of mourning. Hamlet has succeeded in building a new masculine order- with men like himself, Horatio, and Fortinbras in charge. But the moment is fragile, and we know the conquering Fortinbras is no philosopher king.

Hamlet's last action is not to mourn, not to explore the meaning of events, not to examine his inner life, but to behave like Claudius, in his objective decision-making. He sets his election on Fortinbras, the tough, avenging son, and tells Horatio to vindicate his honor publicly, telling the world what really happened. Like Hamlet in Act I, Horatio goes out to join history, having been given a task by a dead man. He gives Hamlet a warrior's funeral, though ironically, Hamlet was a failed warrior, totally unlike his father, until the last minute, when his mother was physically taken from him, and he knew he could never get her back. The same weeds that choked the drowning Ophelia choke Hamlet. Hamlet could not play the man and weed the "rank unweeded garden" of the state. Some "vicious mole of nature" in him, which was his from birth, and of which he was not guilty, drew him down to death. His reason was too absolute and became its opposite, madness. He let love become its opposite and turn to hate.[24] Anything rather than grow up and split with the parental death-grip. Anything rather than see that the problem was not in the stars but in himself. Othello suffers from the same terminal disease.

To the end, Hamlet is reluctant to opt for the world of intrigue, practicality, and control. He dies with relief, never having to admit that the frailty of woman was his own and that Claudius, not his own father, was his shadow, his ghost-shadow, his real father, ambivalently grieved, ambivalently loved. His mourning is not complete; his maturation is aborted. The object of his desire is never made conscious, and he is left a mystery to us and to himself.

Chapter Two

Othello

Two loves I have of comfort and despair,
Which like two spirits do suggest me still.
The better angel is a man right fair,
The worser spirit a woman, colored ill.
To win me soon to hell, my female evil
Tempteth my better angel from my side,
And would corrupt my saint to be a devil,
Wooing his purity with her foul pride.
And whether that my angel be turned fiend
Suspect I may, but not directly tell;
But being both from me, both to each other friend,
I guess one angel in another's hell:
Yet this shall I ne'er know, but live in doubt,
Till my bad angel fire my good one out.
                    Shakespeare, *Sonnet 144*

Like the music of the Elizabethan galliard, alternating quick and slow steps, major and minor keys, Shakespeare's Sonnet 144 contrasts two opposites which are both unified and antagonistic, suggesting an ambivalent universe. Staying in balance and harmony requires that both sides—angel and devil—must be recognized, accepted, and integrated. To achieve what Jung called "integration" we must become conscious that within ourselves we have combined the opposites and need no longer project our personal devil onto others. Hamlet went to the grave incomplete, never conscious of the inner warfare between masculine and feminine. He was never aware that he projected the weakness "that might trouble the heart of a woman" onto the women in his life. Had he married Ophelia, he might have ended by doing to her what Othello did to Desdemona. Murdering the anima or the shadow is a form of suicide, an act Hamlet toys with and Othello actually performs rather than face the ambivalent music of yin and yang and admit the civil warfare of intuition and intellect that tears apart their own psyches.

Two ideologies clash in this play, as happened in *Hamlet*: the traditional, symbolic world order opposes the modern, individualistic, anarchic one. In historical terms, monarchy is being replaced by the capitalistic version of democracy. Literary criticism imitates this same split: romantics and structuralists search for an objective, absolute meaning for a text, while revolutionary deconstructionists like Derrida, in *Of Grammatology*, claim objective knowledge is an illusion, for another text is invented in the act of knowing the first one. Each era thus recreates the text in its own image, as occurred in the eighteenth century, when Shakespeare offended the prevailing ideas of decorum.

The orderly structures of eighteenth-century critics like Samuel Johnson were threatened by the luxuriant excesses of Shakespeare's language. Johnson felt that a stable society required unambiguous prose to defend it. Spontaneity was all very well, but in the interests of a new, more precise and scientific age, a one-to-one correspondence was needed between words and things. When Boswell, his emotional young biographer, took him out to enjoy the sublimity of caves and mountains, Johnson insisted on carrying along a cane with feet and inches marked on it, so as to measure and thus control the excesses of nature. If you allow figurative language to run riot, the thinking went, you would soon experience disorders of reference, identity, and even gender. Shakespeare's language sabotages the neat, necessary social order that keeps reason in charge. In fact, Johnson labelled such sabotage "feminine." Shakespeare's metaphors, seductive as Cleopatra, Johnson wrote, undermine the straightforward Roman manliness of the warrior Marc Antony and the masculine social construct he represents. Shakespeare, then, seemed to be using sensual feminine language to seduce us into another way of being than society upholds as useful and honorable.

In our own century, A. C. Bradley, in *Shakespearean Tragedy*, saw Othello as Othello saw himself, a much-put-upon hero, who was essentially an idealist. F. R. Leavis, a tough-minded realist, attacked Bradley in *A Common Pursuit* for sentimentality, saying Othello was a weak, self-pitying, potential villain, all too ready to accept Iago's hateful hints. Strangely enough, Leavis is acting out Iago's cynical role in relation to the idealistic Bradley, who is playing out the role of a noble but naive Othello.

Deconstructionists like Derrida point out that critics often reenact the neurotic symptoms of the characters they discuss, in what Freud called "secondary revision," aimed at getting a fit between "manifest and latent sense." In the process, they repress and distort the primary experience. Leavis points out in just such distortion in Bradley and goes to Othello's inflated, self-pitying rhetoric to prove his point. Bradley thought Othello a high-minded, innocent poet; Leavis thinks him a pompous liar. Bradley is a romantic, a spokesman for idealism and the innate purity of human nature; Leavis is a spokesman for a cynical, realist-reductionist ideology. Each critic sees what his age demands that he see. In short, critics avoid their own biases with talk, just as Othello rhetorically evades the truth of his own guilt.

The idealized, symbolic world of the traditionalists clashes with the world of ordinary experience, and the clash is echoed in the rhetoric of Shakespeare's drama. Conflict between ideology (thinking) and syntax (feeling) is at the heart of both *Hamlet* and *Othello*. Shakespeare acts out for us the crisis of his age, the conflict between a classical-medieval, hierarchical model of the world, and the new model, which is relativistic, democratic, and individualistic. The conflict can be reduced to the following polarities.

Othello's Worldview:	Iago's Worldview:
idealistic	realistic
symbolic	practical-relativistic
traditional-tribal	individual
static	fluid
aristocratic	democratic
rhetoric (inflated)	"honest" speech

In short, Othello is the past; Iago is ourselves. Shakespeare documents in *Othello* the collapse of the symbolic model and the rise of Iago's centrifugal, destabilizing rhetoric, signalling the shift to a new, syntagmatic model.

Desdemona's world is the feminine counterpart of Othello's. It is characterized by domesticity, family, shared power, acceptance, obedience, relationship, courtly love, cultivated behavior, and forgiveness. Her worldview is not a serious option in the play for men at war, caught up in the transition from a medieval symbolic world to a modern realist one. The gradual breakdown in Othello's mind and language reenacts the displacement of the medieval world by the modern.

In the language of the play, a pattern of disjunction appears, particularly when Iago speaks. He says, "I know my price, I am worth no worse a place/But he. . .," placing first and third person pronouns into opposition. A basic opposition of the play thus emerges: I versus him, them, and everyone else. The opposition is one of rank and race, elect and doomed, and is rooted in predestination, puritanism, and capitalism. Iago (serendipitously similar to 'ego'), is a calculating individual who resents his exclusion from traditional aristocratic society. He is a marginal person, able to succeed only by luck and hustling. A class of men like him appears in the commercial, Renaissance world that replaced the familial, tribal order of the Middle Ages. To survive, Iago has to kill off the idealists and aristocrats, hoist them with their own petard.

Iago dissimulates and lies, as the one on the bottom social rung must often do in order to survive and get ahead. Iago says, "I am not what I am" (I,ii,62). He is a prisoner of his own imagination; he is a non-being, i.e., has no place in the social order. Two rhetorical modes operate in this play: Othello is coming from an idealized reality when he uses his hyperbolic rhetoric, saying he is a public figure, while Iago says *he* is "nothing." Iago, the realist, mirrors idealistic Othello with negation. Iago refuses to sacrifice himself to ideology, word, or God. Like Satan, he will not serve. He is the shadow, the demonic aspect of Othello. They are linked in a death grip like Hamlet's with his stepfather.

If Hamlet had had no conscience, Iago is the man he might have been. Like Claudius, who was Hamlet's shadow, Iago is Othello's, though without love for a woman to soften and humanize him. Unlike Claudius, Iago works in the moment and is poor at strategy, though he is skilled at tactics. He distorts and uses the immediate event. When Cassio paddles fingers with Desdemona, Iago assumes seductive intent. When he thinks Othello is having sex with Desdemona, he says they're "making the beast with two backs." He is a cynical modern man, knowing the price of everything and the value of nothing. The romantic and primitive Othello is no match for him but easily falls into Iago's version of the world, which is similar to the one Shakespeare himself expressed in Sonnet 144.

The sonnet's diction could be Othello's own: angel turned fiend, saint corrupted to devil. Othello has fought off marriage until middle age, opting for the warrior's world. He's good at killing and easily mistakes sentimentality for real feelings. His soldierly self-control gets him admiration and promotion to high station. He has denied his feminine qualities, such as vulnerability, and repressed them into his unconscious, where they form an anima figure easily projectable onto Desdemona. Jung sees such projection as a marriage to the negative, shadow side of one's anima. Othello feared his capacity for tenderness as a fatal weakness. The negative side of this longing for intimacy was the desire to swallow up and control the lover in the name of love.

Othello, of course, is not conscious of any such weakness, having a habit of remaking reality in the image of his dreams.

Although Othello wants to believe he fits in with Desdemona and her aristocratic Venice, the truth is that he's a stranger, an interloper in a civilized world, where perfumed fops dance the galliard, bore strong-blooded females like Desdemona, and rely on tough black mercenaries to do their masculine duty for them. Then the vets come home, try to settle down, and instead blow up, suffering from post-traumatic shock, seeing flashbacks of blood and violence. The more firmly set such a hero is in his masculine role, the more adapted he has become to the warlike world of men, the more Jung says his anima will dominate his unconscious.

What would we expect Othello's anima to look like? She would be young, white, obedient, because he's an "old, black ram." She would be civilized, debonair, courteous, because he is a soldier from a barbaric culture who has risen in the ranks. She would be a singer, because he does not care for music, and orderly because he is a master of the supreme disorder, war. She would love where he hates, forgive where he seeks revenge. If Desdemona had not existed, Othello would have had to invent her.

The anima is an archetype that draws man into both evil and good. She's the intersection of the personal and transpersonal. When she appears in a man's life, he is probably shifting from conscious control by the ego to allowing the unconscious to surface. Jung reminds us continually that only primitives like Othello have access to those deep areas of the unconscious which must be integrated for full maturation, for individuation, and for art. Although Othello claims to be an inarticulate oaf (I,iii,92), he is a consummate poet and storyteller, skilled enough to win Desdemona by his tales. He is evidence in support of Jung's belief that the value of a work of art lies in its acting out of our descent into the unconscious and our surfacing with vital intelligence.

In Jung's view, the shadow must be recognized and incorporated before the anima. And the anima is then incorporated in two ways: before the age of forty, it is a guide to relatedness, while after that age, it leads a man to integration and maturation. Othello is middle-aged and is faced with both goals at once. He avoids the demand and instead integrates only the shadow, Iago, without acknowledging the need for a partner of the opposite sex, that is, for an anima figure:

> I should like to emphasize that the integration of the shadow, or the realization of the personal unconscious,

marks the first stage in the analytic process and that without it a recognition of anima and animus is impossible. The shadow can be realized only in relation to a partner (of the opposite sex). (*CW* 9ii,22/42)

Had Othello acknowledged the Iago within him, then linked himself with Desdemona, he would not have projected his dark side onto his "good angel" and would have dealt summarily with Iago's slanders.

Shakespeare reverses Jung's pattern, showing us an unconscious male primitive becoming conscious of his own capacity for love and hate, being led, "generalled," by a civilized woman. His anima seems to be what leads him to consciousness, while his masculine shadow, Iago the simple soldier, drags him down into blood and death. Yet Shakespeare is ambiguous here. Throughout the play, Desdemona tries to draw Othello the warrior from his symbolic, traditional, warrior's order into the morass of romantic love and obedience to the heart. As surely as Lady Macbeth, she thus destroys herself and him, which she acknowledges at the end. The motives were different, but Desdemona embodies the myth men tell themselves about women, the myth women themselves cooperate in spreading: that men are guiltless of destroying their women, and women must take the blame on themselves. Battered, codependent women, like Desdemona on her deathbed, are simultaneously forgiving, innocent saints and negative anima figures. When Desdemona ends by blaming herself for what has happened, she is right, for she herself was an animus-dominated woman and chose a killer as mate.

Othello was a man old enough to be her father, and with some of her father's qualities—voyeuristic, jealous, willing to destroy a woman if he cannot wholly have her. Othello should be theatrically made up to look as mature as Desdemona's father, Brabantio, since he is her father's friend, invited to the house as a harmless old fellow, well past courting age. Brabantio had kept his daughter to himself. For this jealous father, Desdemona's elopement with Othello must have been an incestuous nightmare. Desdemona is as much her father's anima as she is Othello's. She is the female who promises everything, being both childlike and wise, chaste and wanton, at least in the eyes of her men. She is both demurely courteous and a rebellious runaway. Like Jung's anima, she is both innocent and flirtatious. We are shown only a few signs of what she would have become, had she lived: she banters with Iago, wanting to hear herself praised in courtly fashion; she paddles fingers with Cassio in the way Hamlet thought disgusting; on her last night, having been slapped and insulted by Othello, she muses to Emilia about how attractive the Venetian envoy is. Perhaps Othello kills her just in time to preserve her fantastic innocence, virtue, and single-minded interest in *him*. Ultimately, he must kill her to preserve her as his anima figure, for she continually threatens to turn into a full-blooded woman.

As always, archetypal images are drunk and disorderly. They upset our ideas of historical development, coming as they do out of the atemporal unconscious, like ghosts popping up through trapdoors on Shakespeare's stage. Civilized Desdemona and barbaric Othello are cheek to cheek. Othello is the unconscious bloody force, while Desdemona is sweetly Christian; Othello is the competent public figure, Desdemona the romantic girl who wants to domesticate and drown him in love. She and Othello's dead mother represent witchcraft, anti-reason, and romantic love. They are in constant battle with Iago, who represents wit or tough, reductionistic realism. Othello is not only the story of a brutal, jealous, romantic warrior, but a symbolic conflict between female and male aspects of the personality. Desdemona is as surely undone by her animus as Othello is by his anima. She is as much the slave of her animus/father, whom we do see, as he is of his anima/ mother, whom we do not. We have to guess what Othello's mother was like. "Give this hanky to your bride," she apparently said, controlling him from beyond her deathbed, hinting that its loss would mean his wife was false (III, iv,70-75).

Othello is another Hamlet, another mother-lover, with his unresolved ambivalence and schizoid inability to love or be loved. He is afraid of both extremes—fear of being swallowed up and fear of being isolated. He is overcome by the primary process thinking characteristic of infants, and by an infantile dependency, which he both clings to and resents. He cannot accept the object of his "love" and cannot integrate the good and bad which he sees in others. So he must play the object splitting, preoedipal game. The opposite sex is either all bad or all good. We either worship the woman or murder her. We want her good qualities—her Venetian cultural veneer, her fascination with our war stories, but we don't want her to tell us what to do, to inflict her needs and feelings on us. Jung writes of marriage: "Although man and woman unite, they nevertheless represent irreconcilable opposites which, when activated, degenerate into deadly hostility" (*CW* 12,144/192). The marriage of Othello and Desdemona is just such a conflict.

A woman allows her male to project onto her what he wants her to be and then wonders why the relationship is a disaster. A profound split is meanwhile going on between her imagination and her body.[1] Desdemona projects onto Othello just such a perfection as she once did upon her doting father, who loved her so much that he died when she left him. What she once gave to her father, she now gives to Othello, who has for her the allure of a father, representing both power and sexuality. She acts out the eternal fascination of a young girl with a father figure: power and sex wrapped up in one. She is enslaved to her own father's idealized projection on her and easily falls into the hands of a demon lover, a man who is equally enslaved to his mother's projection upon him of her desire for control, even at the moment of her death. In order to achieve individuation and maturation, the woman must allow herself to go down into the grave of sex, surrendering all control. The man, who has to take the woman into Hades and psychic completion, must accept the burden of being a metaphoric killer. Women's apparent preference for macho, soldierly men is perhaps a reflection of unconscious desire for this guidance into the mysteries of death.

The marriage of Othello and Desdemona is mythically the symbolic union of Europe and colonial Africa, or in classical terms, Aphrodite and Ares, the virgin and the warrior, absolute poles of masculinity and femininity.[2] Such a marriage represents the impossible marriage of the original bisexual self, Plato's myth in the *Symposium*. We can see it also as the woman's mating myth, depicted on the covers of romance novels. The dark male force who pulls her down into the hell of separation, depression, gloom—that side of herself which must face human isolation, conflict, and win a victory is, in Jungian terms, a dark animus, like Othello. Women who adore the dark lover are Dionysius-possessed and dangerous, for they can worship this male god without losing themselves in relation to an ordinary man. Men are often terrified by such self-possessed women in a state of passion, for they do not control them. Such women mate with bulls and produce minotaurs; they are as surely the brides of death as are the Persephones, only the brides of Dionysius do not return. Like Desdemona, they have no mother to come back to.[3] Their only hope is in wholeness, combining male and female within themselves, in being "fair warriors," continually reborn, impossible to kill. The Dionysian bride is what speaks in the dead Desdemona at the end, not the patient Griselda, the fatuous sap, still the slave of her passion.

The woman who goes from carrier of her father's idealized projections to marriage with a husband who promises perfect union, is called into an illusion that inevitably ends in abandonment. Her mistake is that her own projection becomes her love object, and she recreates herself in the image projected onto her, abandoning her genuine self.

Religions make man in the image of God and woman in the image, or as the anima, of man. Initially the woman accepts her role as adoring handmaid; she even takes the lead in creating a relationship based on her sweet servitude. The more intimate the relation becomes, the harder it is to hold onto the pretense that she is its servant and not its creator. Yet she herself wants to dump her servitude. The very thing that drew the man to marry her is what she knows is a cover-up, a betrayal of her real nature, and she herself sets off the bomb that destroys them both.

Desdemona, far from being a sweet, helpless victim, realizes that she erred by loving a phantom. In Act V, she grieves both for her perfect phantom-lover and for the woman she was when she loved him. She mourns the person she lost in childhood when she set out to please her father and make a liar of herself. Without a strong mother figure, she is at the mercy of the two fathers who have betrayed her.[4] In Ovid's story of the virgin drawn down into sexuality by old Hades, the demon-lover, Persephone sees a red pomegranate, dripping juice and seeds. She innocently eats a single seed of the forbidden fruit and then has to stay in Hades with her dark lover, shadow-brother to Zeus, the sky-father god. In the Orphic tradition, Zeus himself, wearing a serpent costume, gets Persephone to eat the sensuous fruit. The virgin has now experienced sexual ecstasy and no longer belongs to the mothers, to Demeter, and to the daylight world of agriculture. Desdemona/Persephone cannot be kept down on the farm anymore. She has lost her mother, but gained herself, or at least the potential to be herself. The trouble is, she falls desperately in love with Hades, her animus, her unknown male self, who happens in this case to be Othello the Moor. Desdemona has become addicted to Othello. She hated the perfumed darlings of the court who peddled their clichés and opportunistic proposals. Desdemona sensed that her animus was not like them. He was a brooding, poetic Heathcliff, a dark warrior from the underworld, accustomed to staking all in battle. Hades the archetype, Beauty's Beast, is both rich and isolated; he has turned from the noisy, productive, outer world toward the subjective inner one. Othello/Hades is both rapist and teacher-father, acting out an incestuous initiation, instructing the woman in the way to her dark, depressed, brooding, violent side.

And what myth is Othello himself living out? For one, the fall of primitive, innocent man into civilized deceit. For another, the story of Cain and Abel, Osiris and Set, the story of Gilgamesh, the fierce, unfeeling Sumerian king, and Enkiddu, his gentle, spiritual brother. When we talk about Othello, we are also talking about Iago, for the two, put together, make one man. Both have a bent for theatrics; both are touchy, wanting to blame and punish others, thinking they are morally superior. Both hate themselves and are unable to love anyone else. As Jung writes in *Aion*:

> Very often the ego experiences a vague feeling of moral defeat and then behaves all the more defensively, defiantly, and self-righteously, thus setting up a vicious circle which only increases feelings of inferiority. . .(making) mutual recognition impossible, and without this there is no relationship. (*CW* 9ii, 9/17)

Othello's self-hatred and inability to admit his fear of inferiority, even to himself, prevent a marriage of true minds with Desdemona. The only person he can marry is his shadow, Iago.

Othello resists confronting his basic conflict, which would, according to Marie-Louise von Franz, "be the end of the ego with all its blather."[5] In *The Psychology of the Transference*, Jung says of a consciousness inflated by projections that it cannot learn from the past or understand the present. As the ego is inflated, it regresses into unconsciousness. The positively inflated ego is swollen with megalomania; the negatively inflated ego experiences annihilation. These two conditions alternate in Othello (*CW* 16,262/472). As in Jung's pattern, both Othello and Iago worship the single image of ego, on which they are fixated, with a profane ritual. Changing the object of worship from profane to sacred, from ego to divinity, is so painful it feels like death. In the case of Othello, it *is* death.

Othello, the warrior, is at war with his own desire for love and peace. To return to the lap of his wife is to return to anonymity, powerlessness, and public ignominy. A return to the mother would mean the loss of male autonomy and a step backward to Hamletism. The first words we hear Othello say (I,ii,20ff) are a boast of his service to the state. They need me, he says. I'm tough. In my country, I come from important people. "But that I love the gentle Desdemona, I would not my unhoused free condition/Put into circumscription and confine for the sea's worth." In other words, this GI is not exactly marriage material. He says more in these lines about how much he loves his freedom than how much he loves his wife. We shouldn't be surprised when later he accepts Iago's idea that courtly love, far from ennobling a man, destroys him.

Othello is a public figure who sees himself playing out his drama on the grand stage. He is at the same time a killer-lover, a prince who is dependent on the mother's approval. As Marion Woodman says of the Prince Charming, he's "unaware of his ambivalence toward women. He hates the woman who makes him feel vulnerable,"[6] yet walks at the edge of an abyss, close to the unconscious, the territory of the destroying witch. Mythically speaking, Othello is an innocent Adam, tempted by the serpent Iago, though he thinks he's being tempted by Eve. Ultimately he betrays his savior, his anima, the one who gives events in his life the dimension of soul. He betrays his straight-shooting Artemis figure, who would help him rediscover his connectedness to her and the rest of humanity. Desdemona, like Othello's mother, represents for him witchcraft, anti-reason, romantic love, and she is in constant battle with Iago, who represents wit or tough, reductionistic realism.

In the outside world, Venice has been attacked by barbarian Turks, as Desdemona is "attacked" and won by the wild Othello. Despite Othello's victorious defense of Venice against the Turks, he must swagger and boast, countering his fear of inferiority. Appearance is everything with Othello. Even after he has murdered his wife in the last act, he boasts of the service he has done the state. Like Hamlet at the end, his primary concern is for his reputation. When the play begins, we see Venice dependent on him for the defense of Cyprus against the thieving Turks. Venice is Desdemona; the Turk is Othello. At the end of the play, when Othello kills himself, he tacitly acknowledges himself a Turk, even while proclaiming his innocence of the murder, projecting his guilt onto Iago.

We see him doing the same thing while protesting his innocence to the duke in Act I. Guilty of stealing Brabantio's young daughter? A child-molester? Not me. She asked for it. Brabantio kept inviting me over to tell war stories, and Desdemona listened in, "greedy. . .to devour up my discourse." She wished "heaven had made her such a man" and said that such a man could woo her. His only witchcraft, Othello asserts, is to use Desdemona's desire for adventure and her compassion against her own best interests. But war stories and pity are not the most auspicious beginning for a marriage.

Until now, we have left out Othello's shadow, Iago, from the union of Othello and Desdemona. Iago is not merely the villain, but Othello's catalyst for growth into honesty and self-awareness. He is the shadow awaiting acknowledgment after Othello married his anima. Honest Iago was right beside Othello all the way up the military ladder. He is a man's man, excellent at tactics, terrible at strategy. He flies by the seat of his pants, staying in the moment, unaware of passing time, but supremely aware that he wants to destroy all that does not feed his hungry ego.

Part of Iago's fury against Desdemona is that he knows Othello is trying to join her world and leave the warrior one where Iago and Othello had been brothers, married on the battlefield. Iago represents himself as a tough, cynical realist, but like all skeptics, he's an idealistic egotist at heart—sentimental, overridden by passion, his judgment derailed by his wounded pride and his jealousy. He is angry that Othello has gone Hollywood and given the lieutenancy to that charming, courtly twit, Cassio.

Iago follows Othello compulsively, wanting something from him that Othello will not give. He loves Othello when Othello hates and hates Othello when Othello loves. Iago is obsessed also with Cassio, whom he thinks Othello loves, and by Desdemona, whom he knows Othello loves. He feels himself inferior to the elegant Cassio and to Desdemona and is angry that "Preferment goes by letter and affection and not by old gradation," meaning that the loyal warhorse has been dumped in favor of a handsome young courtier who can enhance Othello's social image as Iago never could.

Early in the play Iago lets us know who he really is: Othello's second self, his shadow. "In following him, I follow but myself" (I,i,62). Iago is what Jung calls "that hidden, repressed, for the most part inferior and guilt-laden personality whose ultimate ramifications reach back into the realms of our animal ancestors (*CW* 9ii, 266/422). When Jung says "the meeting with oneself is at first the meeting with one's own shadow," he tells us what Iago is to Othello—not an enemy merely, as he has always been seen, but an opportunity to become authentic. Iago is a Caliban who is never acknowledged, a lover who is never embraced. We are given only hints about this phantasm who haunts the play as old Hamlet's ghost haunted his son, urging him to avenge, to murder, and to rejoin the warrior's world of the primitive past.

The warrior's world in which Othello and Iago are at home is violent and loveless, a world in which Desdemona is an intruder. The warrior cannot fall in love and remain a warrior. Jung tells the story of Indians who circled around a naked, beautiful young girl in a prebattle ritual. Whoever had an erection was disqualified from the warpath. Iago consistently tries to keep Othello in the warrior's camp, away from love. When Othello is presumably about to go to bed with his bride, Iago puts the jealous Rodrigo up to a street brawl, which calls out Brabantio in search of his runaway daughter. Amidst the racket and confusion, Iago's favorite milieu, he tells Brabantio that the devil is about to make him a grandfather. Though Desdemona's father indignantly rejects the idea that his house is a barn, Iago insists that his daughter and the Moor were even "now making the beast with two backs." Iago refers often and scurrilously to animals and parts of the body. For him, bodily contact, whether in sex or battle, is raw, violent, and vulgar. Iago seems caught in a twisted version of a child's worldview. His ego tests reality on a primitive level and is what Freud described as primarily "a bodily ego."

Iago's rhetoric becomes particularly gross when he describes women or sexuality, while his references to male concerns such as money, warfare, and power are couched in a more abstract and objective language, one that is less emotionally charged. He describes his own philosophy in I,iii,351-3:

> If the balance of our lives had not one scale of reason to poise another of sensuality, the blood and baseness of our natures would conduct us to most prepost'rous conclusions. But we have reason to cool our raging emotions, our carnal stings, our unbitted lusts.

Throughout the play, he represents himself as Othello's reasonable side, assuming that Desdemona is on the side of blood and baseness, as was the "bad angel" of Sonnet 144. Jung writes of the erotic instinct that "it belongs. . .to the original animal nature of man. . .[yet is] connected with the highest forms of the spirit. But it blooms only when spirit and instinct are in true harmony" (CW 7,28/32). Iago, however, polarizes his opposites rather than harmonizing them and teaches Othello to do the same.

The thought of Othello and Desdemona making love obsesses Iago, for he fears that once the marriage is consummated, he will lose Othello absolutely. He attributes far greater power to Desdemona than she actually has, calling her the "general's general." His fear is that Othello will lose his taste for killing, the act which had previously married him to Iago and will again, in the third act of the play. Murder is mythically a rite of marriage between male opposites, as men on the battlefield well know. Like Cain with Abel, Gilgamesh with Enkiddu, Set with Osiris, Iago means to force the gentle brother, Othello-in-love, into confrontation. In drama, the death of the good brother shocks the audience with recognition and catharsis. We see our own shadow, pretending to be reasonable, seducing us to death. Iago is a parody of the ego, persuading and rationalizing, but his goal is not survival. As Neumann in *The Origins and History of Consciousness* writes, "Only by making friends with the shadow do we gain the friendship of the Self."⁷ The shadow instructs us in how to integrate the positive characteristic of which it is the negative. The cruelty of the shadow is also a measure of its capacity for constructive, righteous anger and for the ability to act promptly, coolly, and decisively. If we fail to see the positive side of the shadow and let it lead us into darkness, we disintegrate into chaos, rather than integrate harmoniously.

When Othello follows his shadow Iago into jealousy, hatred, and violence, he falls apart. He begins to speak the language of the unconscious, which has no syntactical rules, just as dreams, also products of the unconscious, have no logical ones. When Othello breaks down, his poetic language dissolves into nonsense; he does not become rational like Iago. He ends by being only half a man. If the complete Self had won, the shadow (Iago) and the ego (Othello) would have been integrated. For that to occur, Othello would have had also to integrate his anima, Desdemona, as well as confronting his shadow. Without Desdemona, he is helpless; "chaos has come again."

Without Desdemona, her father is likewise in darkness and confusion, carrying a taper as he looks for her, just as Othello carries a taper into the darkness of their marriage/death chamber. "Gross revolt" has taken place; a daughter has rebelled against her father and married a barbarian. When the order of things is thus disturbed, chaos has indeed come again and the dividing line between men and beasts is blurred. Civilized Venice is now at the mercy of the wild Turk—metaphorically, of Othello himself.

Brabantio cannot bear losing his daughter, his anima figure, whom he has jealously guarded from every male who comes near her. In his anguish and fury, he prefigures the Othello of Act III, as does Rodrigo, the jealous suitor. Desdemona is surrounded by marauding Turks; she is every man's anima. And each man who wants her dies, because he insists on control of her and is incapable of loving her for the woman she is. Brabantio will not share his daughter with her husband, though she reasonably points out to him that her own mother transferred her loyalty from father to him. But Brabantio will not give up his territory. He had thought it was safe to bring Othello to his house and let him talk with Desdemona. Who would have thought old Othello would have molested my little girl? Alackaday, who would be a father? Othello must have gotten her drunk, put a spell on her, given her mescaline brownies.

Othello calls Desdemona to witness his innocence. He is only a rough soldier, he says with suspect modesty, and cannot speak like a courtier. He wagers his life on her testimony. If he can't rely on

52

Desdemona, he's had it, Othello is saying. He is righter than he knows. When he lets his Desdemona side speak for peace, saying, "Put up your bright swords or the dew will rust them," Othello speaks with grace, nobility, and effectiveness. When he speaks with Iago's lewd, cruel, soldier's voice, crying for blood and cold reason, Othello leaves the world of Desdemona, the world of possible integration and wholeness, for the adolescent world he and Iago share. In Act I, however, he is still the lover and poet who is one with Desdemona, his defender and his civilized guide. He relies on her to initiate him into the subtlety and complexity of Venetian society.

Desdemona, unknown to Brabantio, has picked up a few pointers from her dark animus. Is she, in fact, the sweet, obedient girl Brabantio described to the duke? Not at all. When she comes on the scene, she is in charge, having been to an empowerment workshop or two. Her father and her childhood are cast away, and Desdemona is now a wife. As soon as she announced her new status and loyalty in a bold speech that cleverly sets her rebellion in the respectable light of wifely loyalty, the duke sends Othello to Cyprus to wipe out the thieving Turks. Challenges to authority are flaring on both the domestic and the national scene. Fine, Othello agrees, without so much as a nod to his bride. I'm out of here. By the way, would you keep an eye on Desdemona while I'm at the front?

Meanwhile Desdemona is looking back and forth at these men—her father, who's just disinherited her, the duke, who's assigned her husband to an overseas tour of duty instead of a honeymoon, and her husband, who has put her on hold for the duration of the war. Just a minute, she says. Just a minute. Why do you think I got married? To live with the Moor, that's why. I love his valiant parts, his soldier's side and I'll be damned if I'll stay behind, a moth of peace, giving up my honeymoon while he goes off to war. It is perhaps the boldest speech of any woman in all of Shakespeare, bolder than Miranda's in *The Tempest*, when she offers to carry Ferdinand's logs and go with him as a servant, if he will not have her as a wife.

Othello backs Desdemona up weakly, not wanting anybody to think he would rather make love than fight. Send her along as baggage, he says, but just to please her. I don't need a honeymoon. I'm all business (I,iii,290). I'm a mature fellow and only trying to guide this young lady's intellectual development.[8] "Let housewives make a skillet of my helm," if romance could keep me from my duty. Later Iago mocks even the best of women as doing little in life but chronicling small beer. The domestic, private world of the maternal eros is nothing to these men. Warrior though she is, Desdemona will never make a dent in their closed ranks, but she's too brash and animus-ridden to know it. Like any young girl who has an older man eating out of her hand, she feels her power and is intoxicated by it.

The world of men is far more complex than Desdemona knows. "Love conquers all" is her motto, straight out of Ovid. Unlike Emilia, Iago's wife, she has no experience with sex, with her own dark side. But she'll learn fast. Her once-doting father's parting shot to his new son-in-law is, watch out for this bitch. She's betrayed me and probably will do the same to you. What does Othello do in answer? He leaves Desdemona in the charge of Iago, his shadow. The marriage is still not consummated. Othello has a war to fight and Desdemona can wait.

Critics have wondered if Othello may have some doubts about whether or not he can satisfy his excited young wife. Shakespeare leaves the consummation of the marriage deliberately ambiguous. Apparently Othello has kept a tight lid on his feelings for years and has lived only around men. He knows more about walking the ramparts like old Hamlet's ghost than about pleasing a woman. A Claudius he's not. He is more like a neurotic described by Jung as fearing sexual inadequacy and experiencing a divided ego, with boundless desire on one hand and loathing of being a slave to love on the other. Othello the nervous bridegroom bolts in the direction of his known expertise—off to war.

His shadow, Iago, speaks for him, in another context: "Ere I would say I would drown myself for the love of a guinea hen, I would change my humanity with a baboon...We have reason to cool our raging motions," he says to the lovesick Rodrigo."Be a man...put money in thy purse." Iago is one of Shakespeare's rootless, commercial men, without loyalty to anyone but himself. Antonio, Prospero's brother in *The Tempest*, also was outside the symbolic order of the traditional past. Both he and Iago are Machiavellian types, turning whatever practical trick they can to advance themselves. They are the new entrepreneurs, the corporate raiders of the day. Iago confesses the secret of such men on the make, as of himself and Othello, when he says, "I never found man that knew how to love himself." Will is more important to him than love, self-interest than self-surrender. What Iago is saying is that he knows he's a despicable man, but that's how all men are—out for themselves. Conduct your business, he tells Rodrigo, as though you're in a jungle, for you are.

Iago intuits Othello's likeness to himself, for all the Moor's fine poetic prattle. He reassures Rodrigo that these Moors are fickle, and so are Venetians. Swingers, is what they are. Don't count on fidelity between an "erring barbarian and a super-subtle Venetian." Instead, put ducats in your purse. Bet money on their breaking up. Iago knows all about changeableness, for he is married to a woman who finds him repulsive and who toys with the idea of taking a lover. He and his wife have the sort of marriage he expects Othello to have. Iago thinks Othello has been sinning with Emilia behind his back, or at least, he says, other people think so, which for him is the same thing. He equates "she seems guilty" with "she is guilty." Image is all, for Iago and Othello. They are merely public men, more concerned about their "bubble reputation" than about the real women they are married to. Othello is still naive, a barbarian soldier who doesn't know zip about Venetian trickery, Iago tells us. So his free and open nature will be that much easier to subvert. Othello is quick to believe men honest, to take the rough, soldier's view of the female, as Cassio does of Bianca. For the men in the play, a woman is someone to use, abuse, and abandon. But they can neither abandon their own wives nor control them. Murder, then, becomes the perfect consummation of marriage, and these two warrior-husbands, Iago and Othello, are professional killers.

Iago's plan is unclear, even to himself. He just does his damage any way he can, like a termite. As we have noted, Iago is a great tactician, but a poor general. Othello had reason to dump him for Cassio, an act which is the proximate cause of Iago's desire for revenge. Pretty soon he's talking not only about getting revenge on Cassio for displacing him, but on Othello, for cuckolding him, though he has no proof. Not until Rodrigo may tell all he knows is Iago committed to the death. What starts as a game draws in the trickster more than he'd bargained for. Ultimately, he must kill Rodrigo, or Rodrigo will spill the spaghetti. As with Hamlet, events pull Iago on, and he is in control of a lot less than he thinks. Everything depends on Othello being another Iago. And Iago intuits that he can trust Othello's basic sickness of soul, because both of them are sick with the same disease. Iago knows Othello as he knows himself; they are functions of the same person.

Although Iago is quick to admit his rascality, he knows as little about his real motives as does Othello. Self-knowledge is not much studied at military school, where both have had their education. For one thing, Iago does not know he loves Othello as much as he hates him, just as Hamlet did not know how much he still loved Gertrude. Now, Iago's love for Othello may be an arguable point, but they are clearly one person in this play. They share the same fundamental emotions—self-hatred and jealousy, which at the root, are one thing. Why does a person who hates himself feel jealous? His logic is irrefutable, given the initial premise of self-loathing: she couldn't love someone as worthless as I, let alone have sex with such a scoundrel, therefore she's no good and is probably having sex with everybody, damn her to hell. So Othello's thoughts run, as do his shadow's. Iago is sure Emilia is unfaithful, and she probably is. He's bitter, defensive, retreating behind cynicism so as not to show his feelings. The worst cynic is a disappointed idealist, said La Rochefoucald, who was probably talking about himself. And perhaps Iago was once as naive as Othello, as idealistic about high-born women as is Cassio. We see only what he has become, the shadow of the warrior, the side of Othello that cannot love or be loved, who is threatened by the feminine to the extent that he must kill it or be killed by it.

Here Shakespeare touches us all where we live. At the point where we separate from each other and lose the potential of maturation, sinking instead into self-hatred, we crave another person who will complete us with his/her perfection. And the same drive will make us hate the one we loved as we hate ourselves—for failing to be perfect.

While the male is seeking union with the perfect Other, who ideally will draw him into spirit, the woman is "increasingly aware that love alone can give her her full stature" (CW 10,130/269). As we've seen with Desdemona/Persephone, the woman is carried into the underworld by the sex act. A common Elizabethan metaphor equates sex with death. As in Sonnet 144, the private parts were a "hell" or, if we go back to the Persephone myth, Hades. The woman who lost her virginity did in fact risk death. She stood a good chance of becoming pregnant, since Ortho was not yet in business, and, in a time of primitive, unsanitary medical care, she might well die in childbirth. The man compensated her for these risks by protection in marriage. Or so the social contract went. Those who break the rules, as Desdemona does by disobeying her father, and as Othello does by breaking faith with his wife, are doomed.

Death and sexuality run rampant in the play, uncontained by the ritual they defy, as was the case in Hamlet. Kerenyi, in Essays on a Science of Mythology, cites the close association of wedding feasts and funeral feasts.[9] Both are marked by laments and obscene remarks, of which there are plenty in Act I. Marriage is both a prelude to birth and an invitation to death. When Desdemona lays out her wedding sheets, she is also dimly aware that she is preparing her burial shroud. Othello will murder her on her marriage bed, then die melodramatically upon a kiss, paying for his crime with his life. For this demon-lover, this initiator of Persephone into Hades, his chief problem is his own guilt. He is unsure that he's good enough for his noble wife and is aware that she has a rapport with the Venetian aristocracy that he lacks. She is able to speak before the duke, while he is too rough a soldier to defend himself. He has finally arrived in society but can think of no reason that Desdemona might have married him except pity. He believes the only reason Venice rewards him is that the city needs his barbarian sword arm. Later he's proved right, for the duke sends an envoy to tell him that Cassio has been made the new governor—his rival, Cassio. It's the last straw. When the Turkish fleet is wrecked in the tempest at the beginning of Act II, we see a prefiguring of barbarian Othello's end. Cassio and "the warlike Moor Othello" are separated by the storm, and Cassio makes it to land first, fearing he has lost Othello "on a dangerous sea," which loss is metaphorically about to occur. The tempest is a symbol of the conflict between Othello's shadow and his anima, who are literally in the same boat. The warrior is at war within himself. If no battle is going on outside, he must face the interior one.

This tempest, like Prospero's, is a metaphor for the inner conflict between a man's public image and his private view of himself as a "poor forked thing," which King Lear calls himself during a rare moment of humility and of insight into his own weakness. The woman, whether Cordelia or Desdemona, daughter or wife, will not let her man get by with believing his own press, and he does not love her the more for her honesty. Othello sees himself with binocular vision—as a man in the public, masculine world and as a boy, floundering in the warm bath of the maternal eros, in danger of drowning. Othello is at home in the warrior's world, and he clearly fears life in the arms of Desdemona, who is carrying his mother's handkerchief, and thus his mother's authority. "The further and the more unreal the personal mother is, the deeper the son's longing plunges into the depths of his soul to awaken her image" (*CW* 13,112/147). For Othello, that image is Desdemona, his good angel, his soul. Yet he is ambivalent toward this feminine side of himself. As a young man, he left the maternal world to be a soldier and has no intention of getting swallowed up again. Iago has little work to convince him that women are not to be trusted. From the beginning, although Othello is unconscious of it, he and Iago are united in a conspiracy against weakening to female seduction. Iago tells Othello only what Othello wants to hear.

Cassio, the touchstone for truth in the play, gives an alternate, healthy reading of the marriage, just so the audience will understand how far off the wall Othello is. In II,i,85ff, Cassio expresses the relief of all Venetians that soldierly Othello and the "divine Desdemona" will prove a metaphor for civic health, renewing Venice's "extinct spirits" as the hero makes "love's quick pants in Desdemona's arms." Note the beat of the line, its stressed, impassioned single syllables, demonstrating his vicarious excitement. Far from being jealous of Othello, Cassio views the bride and groom as mythical divinities, acting out a ritual that will benefit the state.

Iago, on the other hand, gives us a picture of the private hell which is his idea of marriage: not a union of gods, a fusion of the two sides of the psyche, but a coupling between beasts. In II,i,115, Iago mocks his wife, Emilia, when Cassio kisses her in welcome. Later we learn that Iago thinks the two have kissed before, with rather quicker pants. His words are vicious, but so is the hurt behind them: "Sir, would she give you so much of her lips/As of her tongue she oft bestows on me, You would have enough." He then goes headlong into a diatribe against women, whom he accuses of being publicly innocent while they are wildcats indoors. Desdemona thinks he's kidding and tries to make a game of praising women in the courtly manner. But where she would have him praise, Iago blames. His view of women's duplicity is true, says "Honest Iago," "or else he is a Turk," metaphorically, a betrayer. To Iago, the perfect woman is a bundle of contradictions, and thus impossible. Even those who seem perfect, like Desdemona, cannot be. Iago, who says that he never knew a man who loved himself, can love no one else. If he hates himself, he must hate his female other half, for she must be evil, being human as he is.

Desdemona finds his conclusion "lame and impotent," fighting words for Iago, who talks to himself bitterly after hearing them, muttering about enema tubes and finger kissing. At just this moment, he's decided to make Cassio, beside whom he sleeps in the barracks, the fly in the web being spun for the Moor and his bride. Though we know nothing about Iago's marriage except that he and Emilia hate each other, we may speculate. Did the marriage founder on Iago's impotence? Is Iago really a lover of men, rather than a lover of women? Is all his talk of clyster pipes, trumpets, and the filth of women a testimony to his sexual love for Othello? In any case, Iago's view of the feminine is the mirror image of Othello's exaggerated courtly one.

Othello enters after the shipwreck of the Turks, calling Desdemona his "Fair Warrior," acknowledging her toughness for having come to the front on her honeymoon. His phrase is impersonal and militaristic. She overrides his formal posturing and greets him as the mere man he is, "My dear Othello." For him, she is "the calm" after the storm, without whom chaos will come again (II,i,22 ff). He says some ominous words: nothing better than this moment is likely to come. Remember, he still has not slept with her. Desdemona catches his drift and counters that she expects their love to grow in time. Othello lives in a legendary world, where time has no meaning. He is associated with broad, open space, the area of dream, of the unconscious, while Desdemona, the civilized Venetian, inhabits the world of time and historic memory.

Othello of Act I is on a roll, lyrically in love, gearing up to consummate his marriage. He has the choice before him of moving from war to peace, from polarization to integration, from Iago to Desdemona. "Our wars are done," he says. That's what *he* thinks. When the killing is over, the loving has to start, and Othello isn't ready for the loving. Even as he prattles "out of fashion" to Desdemona, he is nervous about wallowing in unsoldierly ease. Struggling to stay in control, he sends Iago to get his money trunks, his coffers. Iago and the commercial world are the alternative to Desdemona and the intuitive world. If war is not to stand between them, commercial trade will, for in the public, masculine order, commerce is the peacetime equivalent of war. Later, he will mock Desdemona in her bedroom, calling Emilia the bawd who is standing lookout for Desdemona's customers. Marriage will be reduced to a mere commercial transaction, as his Iago-side always believed it was. The mythical exchange of male and female, where the woman lays her life on the line in childbirth and the man defends her with his own life, has been commercialized, turned into an impersonal, feelingless exchange. That is the world Iago would substitute for Desdemona's. Othello must choose between them.

Iago fears his master will opt for the woman. In a fit of jealous rage, he tells Rodrigo that the newly married couple will soon be sated. Desdemona will turn from Othello to a gentleman like Cassio. Rodrigo protests that she is a blessed woman, not a beer hall wench. Iago answers him with words that could be the motto of the play: "If she had been blessed, she would never have loved the Moor" (II,i,283). A few lines later, he admits that he loves her too, not out of "absolute lust." In this speech, he tangles his syntax, following the claim of love with a negation and a qualification, the word "absolute." To complete the disintegration of his syntax, Iago slides in the defensive words, "Though peradventure. . .," leaving Rodrigo and us in confusion as to his meaning.

Even if he does not love Desdemona, Iago says, maybe he is accountable for "as great a sin," one that he is obviously using murky language to cover up. By "loving" Desdemona he may have found a socially acceptable way to admit he loves Othello, with whom he assumes Desdemona is even now uniting. He does not love Desdemona but is jealous of her, as he is of Cassio. In fact, he is jealousy itself and represents Othello's terror of rejection and humiliation, the shadow side of the barbarian warrior's magnanimity and self-confidence.

Instead of acknowledging that he loves Othello, Iago tries to destroy those whom Othello loves. The more he can make another seem despicable, the more he can avoid facing what pains him—his own self-hatred. The old critical saw about Iago's "motiveless malignity" need not be resorted to, if Iago is seen psychoanalytically as acting out the dark, unconscious life of Othello, whose words and actions mirror his shadow's. When Othello arrives on Cyprus, for instance, he uses commercial language, typical of Iago, to announce the coming consummation: "the purchase made, the fruits are yet to ensue; the profit's yet to come 'tween me and you" (II,iii,10-11). Iago remarks to Cassio that Desdemona is "sport for Jove." Metaphors of commerce and gaming come easily to Iago and Othello, as they do not to Cassio. Until he is drunk, Cassio is a courtier and speaks like one. His drunkenness, encouraged by Iago, shows us his cruel, dark side, the same side he later shows when he mocks the devotion of his mistress, Bianca. Iago has a way of bringing out the worst in a man, but we must note that he does not create it.

In II,iii, Othello is once again roused from his marriage bed by one of Iago's fights, or mutinies, as Iago acknowledges them to be. He is in a bad mood, hardly what one would expect after a happy interlude in bed with his hard-won bride. What does he say? I'll kill the next man that moves. As an afterthought, he asks what's going on. Who started this brawl, anyway? As when he suspects Desdemona of adultery, Othello strikes first and asks questions afterward. Othello describes his own flaw: "My blood begins my safer guides to rule." His potential for violence is clear. Maybe he wasn't a soldier in his marriage bed, but by God, here he's in charge. Besides, the island is under threat of war. Othello has a public duty to do, always something he prefers over private pleasure. The next thing we see is Othello firing Cassio, even while he says he loves him: "Never more be officer of mine." Later he will cashier Desdemona the same way, firing his good angel out.

Othello is a creature out of legend, a man of absolutes who is incapable of shades of gray. A woman is either a whore or a saint. A man is a loyal soldier even in his spare time, or he is court-martialled. Again Othello is split-projecting, acting out his own polarization. Desdemona comes on the scene as if to heal the split, her mythical role throughout the play, though Othello refuses to accept it. He sees like an adolescent, always thinking in extremes, and so does Iago.

Iago thinks Desdemona a mysterious goddess, a power figure, whom he is sure Othello loves besottedly. She can do anything with

Othello she wants to, he says in II,iii,350: "Even as her appetite shall play the god with his weak function," (i.e., her will overrides his weakened faculties). Othello is a slave to love, lost to the masculine world of comradeship, bawdy talk, and brave deeds, or so Iago thinks. In fact, Othello is more like his "ancient" than he seems, eager to leave his marriage bed in order to walk the ramparts and dine with his captains. Iago's version of the world increasingly prevails in the play, and we have little doubt which way Othello will turn. He is becoming more and more the lord of Hades, dragging Persephone down to death as Iago increasingly speaks and acts for him. Right after the apparent consummation of the marriage, we see clowns on stage, making dirty remarks about noses, wind instruments, and tails. The play is full of noses and smells, and reference to them is part of an overall reductive pattern. The play sinks from the ethereal heights of courtly love to the gutter, where Iago wants to lead Othello and where Othello easily lets himself be led by the nose.

The crucial event on which the play turns is Desdemona's defense of Cassio, in Act III. Emilia lets us know that Desdemona is speaking up for the ousted lieutenant even before she is asked to help. That's just like the divine Desdemona. Ask her for the time of day and she'll give you her watch. Othello puts Desdemona off, saying he'll take Cassio back in his own time. Since Othello has a primitive sense of time, living as he does in the wide open spaces of myth, he means never—exactly as he said to Cassio. "Never more be officer of mine." Othello didn't get where he is in the army by being nice or reasonable. If a man's out, he's out. That's the end of it. At least, so it used to be, before the general had a general, before he married.

Desdemona is sure she can bring off a reprieve for Cassio, sure of her power, sure she is a warrior. She does not realize that the Iago side of Othello is moving into high gear. At the moment, he's going up to inspect the ramparts (III,iii,25), perhaps signalling a new sense of insecurity, since he and Desdemona have finally made love, as probably they have. He now knows she is a sexy woman and perhaps desires more of him than he wants or is able to give. When Iago says of Cassio, sneaking away from Desdemona, "Ha! I like not that!" Othello is motivated to jump on the hint.

Desdemona, ready for battle after her night of love, puts on the pressure. Take Cassio back, dear. I tell you he's a good man and I know an honest face when I see one. Here's the woman who believes Iago honest to the end. And, Othello might be thinking, the woman who fondly and foolishly thinks he's the catch of the year. Not now, says

Othello. Well, when? demands Desdemona, and by the way, are you eating at home tonight? No, says Othello, I'm dining with my captains at the citadel. Already he's pulling away from her, his Iago side in full tilt, headed for war games. She keeps after him. Tell me when you'll take Cassio back. Tuesday? Wednesday? No more than three days. Here again Desdemona is on the side of time, of history. She wants to pin her wild husband down, assert her reasonableness and her power. "If you asked me anything, would I stand here mamm'ring on?" She's getting a bit shrill and now lays a guilt trip on him, right in front of Emilia and Iago. How mean of you, she complains, to have fired our good friend Michael Cassio, who came courting with you. Desdemona makes a big mistake here, thinking women's rules apply to men's concerns. A general, after all, does not assign a man a lieutenancy because the two went courting together. Desdemona is clearly out of her depth, but she does not know it and plunges bravely on. O fair warrior.

Othello bites his nether lip and gives her the minimum, a "keep quiet," one of Iago's favorite demands of Emilia. Cassio can come when he wants to. "I will deny thee nothing." Desdemona seems to know he is fobbing her off as one would a demanding, unreasonable child, and she's fighting mad: look, when I want something, I want it now. I'm testing your love, is what I'm doing. We've got a serious fight going here, our first one, and I mean to win. Don't patronize me, by God. All right, says Othello, all right. I hear you. Just leave me alone. "Shall I deny you?" she says, leaving. No, I'm all loving obedience, not like somebody I know. She is attempting once again to control him by his guilt. Desdemona has now entered the warrior's world and is playing with every weapon she's got. Something has gone sour, and she seems to sense that her position is not as strong as it was before they went to bed together.

Othello still loves her, we hear him say after she leaves, but he can now imagine not loving her, a time when chaos would come again. He is having trouble organizing himself into Desdemona's civilized, domesticated world and senses the chaos of the battlefield rising in him. Jung says such a man is in danger of losing touch with the "compensating powers of the unconscious," along with his anima. He is subject to fits of rage, to "feelings of inferiority," and to a lack of self-criticism, all of which cause him "to lose touch with reality" (CW 13,335/454-5). As Othello sinks into chaos, out of Desdemona's reach, Iago enters on cue, the tempter in paradise. Act III,iii,115 ff. tracks the efforts of Othello to understand himself, or to understand Iago, which is the same thing. Already it's gnawing on him that Desdemona is only an ordinary woman who enjoyed sex with her husband. The next step is to say that she might enjoy sex with anyone.

Othello's words in III,iii,210 ff. reveal his insecurity and self-doubt: "Nor from mine own weak merits will I draw the smallest fear or doubt of her revolt/For she had eyes, and chose me." Even in the act of saying he has nothing to fear because Desdemona chose him above others, he betrays his fear. She saw what I was, my weak merits, and she married me anyway. Yes, and she deceived her father to do it, Iago mocks him, saying that by loving Othello, Desdemona proved that her judgment was suspect. Iago pushes this point so far that Othello is offended: Desdemona was unnatural in her choice of a mate, and once she compares you to her countrymen, she will be sorry she ran off with you, barbarian that you are. Othello starts to walk out on him, having had enough. It is depressing to hear your shadow telling you you are totally without couth, especially if in your heart of hearts, you believe it.

After Iago leaves him, Othello talks of Desdemona in metaphors that suggest his real idea of marriage, underneath the courtly talk of Act I. He has declined, like the setting sun. She is a hawk, a predatory animal, forcibly strapped to his arm. He has already made up his mind she's false and has turned against him because he's black, has no courtly conversation, and above all is old and sexually wanting. Othello gets to the heart of the marriage dilemma, when he says, "O curse of marriage, that we can call these delicate [delicious] creatures ours and not their appetites." In other words, he is not in control of Desdemona's sexuality, and therefore he assumes he is being betrayed. As Jung writes, such a man has no objective reality against which to match his distorted concept of wife and mother (*CW* 9ii,18/37). Once he gives up his projection, he has no bond with the outside world and is thus fatally alone. Metaphorically, Othello is saying he is abandoned, unloved, ontologically insecure, like all the rest of us, and that he refuses to admit his vulnerability without a fight.

Desdemona perceives his wound and wants to bind it up with his mother's handkerchief. Othello, however, will not accept healing from her hands. He does not trust her, believing that the horns which hurt his head are her fault. In Jungian terms, the anima/mother/wife is rejected, and healthy psychic integration therefore cannot take place. Desdemona is not able to heal his separation from his own feminine aspect, because Iago has wormed his way too deeply into Othello's heart. Othello's unacknowledged shadow has driven him permanently into division, despair, and disharmony. Desdemona's handkerchief is too small to encompass Othello's wide-open spaces, his barbaric, violent, timeless, unconscious world. He doesn't even stop to notice Desdemona is offering him, as a healing talisman, his mother's handkerchief, with its strawberries, which are symbolic of perfect righteousness and of fertility. And Desdemona does not stop to notice that she has lost the handkerchief, because she's too in love with Othello to protect herself. What neither of them remembers and what few critics do, is that *it was Othello who lost the handkerchief, not Desdemona.* He pushes it from her hand, refusing the world of the mothers. No strawberry hankies for him. Later we will read that the other men are not able to get copies of the health-giving handkerchief. They, too, are warriors and stuck in a world where there is no mercy, only blood. Othello will not be bound by Desdemona's love and his mother's handkerchief because his wound is too big, and his desire for an "unhoused free condition" (I,ii,28) is too strong.

Possession and use of the handkerchief determine who holds power in the play. When Desdemona loses it to Iago, he and Othello become more and more the same person. Earlier in the play, Iago used only rough prose. Now he speaks in poetry: "Not poppy nor mandragora, nor all the drowsy syrups of the world shall ever medicine thee to that sweet sleep which thou ow'dst yesterday" (III,iii,373-4). Othello comes in fuming coarsely that Desdemona is false. Better that the whole camp had topped her, as long as he never knew. Now his confusion about time is more obvious. Desdemona's been on Cyprus for less than twenty-four hours, and already he is imagining that she has slept with the whole army. Hyperbole is the linguistic counterpart to Othello's general extremism. The trouble with Othello is that he cannot accept peace and love. If there is no war, his Iago side will create one.

He groans that Desdemona's name is now as black as his face, revealing his own view of himself (ll. 430ff.). He can't stand ambiguities—either Desdemona's pure or she's evil. Either she's the goddess who would redeem and transform him, or she's his bad angel. Iago further confuses the shifting identities in the play when he says he slept entwined with Cassio and was kissed and called Desdemona in Cassio's dream. Iago's own fantasies are running wild now and become Othello's. In fact, during this scene they enter into a marriage that, unlike their unions with women, is of true minds. "O blood, blood, blood," Othello roars as the marriage begins, the marriage of warriors on the battlefield. They kneel before the candles, under the stars, Iago binding himself to be the sword, the phallus, of Othello in this revenge. The two Othellos are now one. Othello has a new general. Symbolically, he restores Iago to his old place as right-hand man, and Iago says like a good wife, "I am your own forever" (III,iii,244).

Just as Othello has polarized his image of Desdemona and now sees her as the wicked witch, Desdemona sees only his good side, his "daddy" side, for he has in her mind replaced Brabantio, the rejecting, "bad" daddy. She tells Emilia that Othello comes from a country where men are godlike, beyond feelings of jealousy. Far from suspecting that Othello now hates her, she says she will not leave him alone for a minute, until he gives in to her and calls Cassio back. Nothing could be less tactful, more aggressive, more of an indictment that she is guilty of trying to take over Othello's life. She is the governor and makes the decisions, not he. Othello counters by telling her she has a hot, moist hand, that is, she's a sexy wench and probably can't be trusted. Now, he says, give me that handkerchief which an Egyptian charmer gave my mother so she could "bend my father to her love," i.e., her will. Without this talisman, the father's eye would rove, and the marriage would be doomed. There is "magic in the web," Othello says. The handkerchief was made by holy worms. He is carried away here by his own hyperbole, telling one fantastic story after another. The handkerchief becomes an "it," a floating signifier, carrying the burden of anything Othello wants to lay on it, meaning anything he wants it to mean.

When Othello walks out in a fury because she cannot produce the handkerchief, Desdemona seems dimly aware that something has gone wrong. She tells Cassio, who is still hoping she has some influence, "my lord is not my lord." For the first time, she begins to see Emilia's point that men are not gods. Othello, she perceives, is angry about something more than the handkerchief (ll. 160ff). She immediately returns, however, to her stubborn view of Othello as perfect—and herself as an "unhandsome warrior," who was too dumb to see he was troubled with affairs of state. Gradually her ignorance of the man's world is dawning on her, and her naive self-confidence ebbs.

Desdemona longs to know Othello fully, and like Psyche bending over Eros with her lamp, she loses him in the very act of intimacy. Othello, like Eros, prefers remaining unknown in the dark and wants his woman to stay out of his business. Between them, Iago and Desdemona, shadow and anima, have cut him in two. Jung wrote in *Symbols of Transformation* about such a person: "So far as his emotional life is concerned, he has not yet caught up with himself, as is often the case with people who are apparently so masterful towards life and their fellows, but who have remained infantile in regard to the demands of feelings" (*CW* 5,284/431). Othello knew no more about women and their feelings than did that other warrior, old Hamlet. Both of them stomp around on the ramparts, crying for vengeance. Both do what Freud said all men do. They displace sex with death. As Daniel Weiss says in *The Critic Agonistes* :

> It is in the nature of the tragic protagonist to be above all else obsessive. And obsession tends. . .to be most obtuse to its own unconscious aims. Obsessive thinking and behavior achieve that interesting compromise that our divided minds are capable of: the mind abandons its sexual designs on the object while continuing to retain the object itself.

For Shakespeare, Weiss says, "murder was a symbolic intensification of a relationship, . . .the psychopathic core of infantile violence."[10] In the case of both Iago and Othello, the choice of a woman is displaced onto a choice for death; both men are wife-murderers. Othello and Iago are not warriors for nothing. Love makes them uneasy; death is familiar and comfortable. Like Hamlet between Gertrude and Claudius, Othello is caught between his anima and his shadow, fighting to maintain his collapsing ego.

Act IV, like most of Shakespeare's fourth acts, is full of darkness, confusion, and menace. Othello's once poetic, graceful speech patterns are breaking down. Chaos has come again, as he foresaw would occur when Desdemona was no longer loved. As Iago talks about Desdemona lying naked in bed with Cassio (IV,i,45), Othello explodes:"Handkerchief-confession-handkerchief. . .Pish! Noses, ears, and lips. . .O devil!" The barbarian in him surfaces. His reason gives way, he falls unconscious. When he wakes, Iago is there to tell him that all men lie in improper beds. Women are the enemy, the devil. Then he says a mysterious thing, a clue to his real inner conflict and Othello's: "Knowing what I am, I know what she shall be." Since he (Othello/Iago) is rotten, so is the woman, because she loves him. Not to know this, not to mistrust women as Iago does, means you're not a man—the last thing Othello wants to hear, having at this point so many doubts of his manhood and his control over events.

Othello has been spending too much time with Iago, who's an expert at dissolving language into nonsense. As soon as Iago sets up one meaning in his monologues, he jumps away from it or shifts it. The moment he gives a reason for his hatred, Iago mentions alternative ones (II,i,286-96). His syntax is oddly decentered and tangled: "I love Desdemona, not from unbridled lust but for revenge," the word *but* leading into the more believable motive. Iago lives continually in the present, flowing from thought to projection, taking advantage of every opportunity, creating opportunities with incomplete suggestions. In III,iii,35-41, for instance, he says: "Ha, I like not that." Othello must react with an attempted completion of the thought: What is it you don't like? Thus Othello is manipulated into taking responsibility for projecting the insinuated guilt. Iago does not specify. Without a single assertion, by using negation, supremely the language of the manipulator, he makes Cassio seem a sneak: "I know not what." Iago is imprisoned in negation, the void and envy of being, the negation of eros. But Othello is likewise imprisoned, in hyperbolic, inflated affirmations. So they both live in unreal worlds: Iago closed to others, in bourgeois isolation, and Othello isolated by his would-be aristocratic exclusivity. Both are strangers to other men and their language communicates with no one.

Othello, even by Act III, has lost his tenuous, desired connection with the civilized Venetian world represented by Desdemona and is talking in broken, surly English, weakly imitating Iago. His moral status has plummeted with his syntax. The symbolic handkerchief of his mother has now been given to a whore, and in Othello's overheated mind, that means his wife is a whore, too. As Marion Woodman says, in *The Pregnant Virgin,* "there is nothing stronger than whore energy to depotentiate the patriarchal collective that has kept the virgin silent."[11] That energy sends the male ego plummeting, stripping away its defenses and initiating it into wholeness, or will, if the whore energy is accepted and not judged and denied, if it is not turned into the devil and rejected.

Othello has a few moments of longing in which he remembers that Desdemona is the traditional Good Woman: she sings, she is witty, she embroiders. "She might lie by an emperor's side and command him tasks" (IV,i,96ff). For a moment Othello is again the man Desdemona married, worshipful as a troubadour. His emotions are not at his command but swing between violent extremes. Jung writes of the inferiorities "that constitute the shadow":

> they have an emotional nature, a kind of autonomy and accordingly an obsessive, or better, possessive quality. Emotion. . .is not an activity of the individual but something that happens to him. Affects occur usually where adaptation is weakest. (*CW* 9ii, 8-9/15)

In Othello's case, the weakest point in his adaptation is his fear that he is not good enough for Desdemona and Venice.

A few words from Iago on the public humiliation of cuckoldry, and Othello moves to the other pole, ready to chop Desdemona "into messes." Cinthio, Shakespeare's source, had Othello bring down the whole house on Desdemona, but Shakespeare is both more credible and more metaphoric than his source. Iago persuades Othello to strangle Desdemona in their marriage bed, in a twisted, sadistic version of the sex act, precisely paralleling the murder to the consummation of their marriage. Othello must take Desdemona/Persephone, the innocent virgin, down into the underworld of terror, violence, loss, and isolation, as the god of death, the dark animus always does and must always do, if the virgin is to become whole.[12]

The long drawn-out death begins with Desdemona's humiliation before the Venetian envoys, those same men who have come to tell Othello he is no longer Governor of Cyprus and that Cassio has taken his place. Othello now knows he's been used by Venice. In his mind Desdemona *is* Venice and has used him. He will have his revenge on her, on Venice, on the whole slick, civilized world.

Alone together, Desdemona and Othello continue their power struggle. He calls her slut; she says she's his wife, just as she called him by his name after he called her a fair "warrior" in better days. Othello resorts to Iago's brothel imagery, for more and more he is, in fact, Iago. Desdemona is now a cistern where toads knot and gender. Othello's crudeness leaves Desdemona stunned, looking on helplessly while he pays Emilia for her service as a bawd. Emilia, whose life with Iago has taught her to pay no attention to men's moods, is not much help. Both women turn to Iago, and for a moment Desdemona manages to shake his cynicism (IV,ii,145). Don't cry, he begs her. When Emilia says that some treacherous scoundrel maligned her to Othello, Iago says, more truly than he knows, "There is no such man," for he is now a nothing, a mere caudal appendage to the rampaging Othello.

"If such there be, heaven pardon him," says Desdemona, stopping Iago in his tracks. He never expected to be forgiven and knows nothing about that divine world out of which forgiveness comes. His cynicism is for a moment dissolved. When Desdemona goes down on her knees to him and begs his help in winning Othello back, Iago tries to squirm away from her hands hanging on him, from her pleading, from her trust in his good will. Go to supper, he says, breaking away. All things shall be well. This moment offers Iago his chance at redemption, and he seems to know it. In the next scene with Rodrigo, Iago is so distracted that he can only offer uncharacteristically weak defenses against Rodrigo's accusations, repeating helplessly, "Very well, very well," or "Go to, go to." Finally Rodrigo threatens to expose Iago's villainy. That threat shocks Iago back into his usual self-seeking, efficient behavior. From now to the end of the play, he is an irredeemable killer.

Desdemona, meanwhile, is moving into a transpersonal state, at the opposite pole from Iago. She has made up her marriage/death bed. When Emilia says any woman would betray a man if the price were right, or in revenge for ill treatment, Desdemona gently sends her away, rejecting her shadow as absolutely as Othello embraces his. She swears the Christian oath, to overcome evil with good. Othello is coming to her door to serve as her judge and then murder her, his opposite, his good angel. The battle lines are drawn.

In the ordinary world outside the rarefied space of the idealist or the cynic, people are a mixture of good and bad, as are Cassio and Emilia. But Othello, Iago, and Desdemona, like Hamlet, are figures out of myth, wandering between microcosmos and macrocosmos. At home nowhere, they are outside history, seeking impossible absolutes. Each extreme brings forth its opposite. Iago, the rigid positivist and behaviorist, creates irrationality and chaos. Othello, the romantic idealist, murders his wife, perhaps because her sexual desire for him made her imperfect. Desdemona, devoted to honesty, purity, and truth, denies to the end that Othello has killed her. Each lives in a private, self-created world, outside the shared one.

The Othellos and Iagos and Macbeths in Shakespeare are humanity gone mad, separated from the harmonious moral/social fabric represented by the Desdemonas. They lack the mother's handkerchief, the capacity for pity, the capacity for love. The handkerchief reminds us of the play's theme: the war between wit and witchcraft, reason and emotion, head and heart. The conflict is characteristic of the age. Othello and Iago reflect the historic intersection of Protestant independent inner life and the new secular nation state with its basis in power, order, and anonymity, the first step toward twentieth-century totalitarian government. Individualism, as Iago, Othello, and later Antonio live it, borrows the worst features of two major Renaissance movements— secular nationalism and Protestant freedom. The individual becomes the power-mad god of his own cosmos and hates the natural order which subordinates him to authority.[6] So he becomes tyrant over a totalitarian state of his own, which Othello does on Cyprus, when his ego becomes tyrant over the rest of his personality. As the ego is to the individual, so is the tyrant to the modern state. Othello is the representative of the self-made man, and Iago is his sword arm. Traditional Elizabethans like Desdemona and Cassio, who believe in fact fused with value, inseparable from it, are doomed, like the young, humanistic libertarians shot down in Tiananmen Square.

The great questions that come up during the last act of the play are as follows. Who rises above the distorted ego-version of events and has a perception? Who takes the step toward maturation, and who fails to take that step? Who defends ego to the death, and who takes responsibility for choices? Let us look first at Othello's action through the last deadly scenes.

Othello has created a screen so that he will never have to know the real truth about himself. He is lawyer, judge, and executioner, though he has no case, no cause. "Insight and good will are unavailing because the cause of the emotion appears to lie, beyond all possibility of doubt in the other person" (*CW* 9ii,9/16). In fact, Othello says, using a characteristically missing signifier, "It is the cause, it is the cause, my soul, Let me not name it to you, you chaste stars." The signifier is floating, as in the case of the handkerchief. It means anything he wants it to mean—her adultery, his inability to hold her, the injustice, the pity of it all. He sees the sleeping Desdemona as evil, yet pure as alabaster. Othello habitually sees perfection as white stone, unchangeable, pure and dead. It's as Poe said: the most beautiful thing in the world is a dead girl. Why? Because she's able to inspire without being able to control. The only safe anima is a dead anima. Even before he kills Desdemona, Othello gets a thrilling rush over how much he's going to love her when she's dead. He "dies upon a kiss." Hamlet's leaping into the grave again, weeping and roaring that he loved the girl he brought down to Hades. Othello, addressing his sleeping wife, remarks that he can't replant the rose once he has plucked it. Is he mourning the fact that he can't make Desdemona a virgin again? That he can't keep her forever pure, unattainable, immature, and powerless? Once she becomes a potential mother, a power in her own right, the game is up. The warrior loses his battle for freedom. And freedom is everything to Othello. He kills himself at the end, rather than lose it.

Desdemona wakes up groggily, asking who's there. Othello? What a question. Who did she think it was? Cassio? If Othello had any last doubts, she has relieved them. Come to bed, she says, giving him a final chance for maturation, toward assimilation of her, his anima and good angel. But Othello will never come to bed again. He does not dare. The more the woman loves, the more the man withdraws. The female's tragedy is her love for a perpetually adolescent, rebellious male who will hate her for loving him. The wedding bed thus becomes an execution place. What dies is the dream of purity, innocence, and divinity projected onto a mere woman. In its place is the real woman with curlers, with requests to take out the garbage and to reinstate one's drunk lieutenant.

Othello decently offers her time to pray. He does not want to send her unprepared soul to hell. Desdemona knows he's no saintly judge, for she sees his eyes rolling, the way he gets when he's in his warrior mode. "Think on thy sins," he insists. And she reminds him: "They are the loves I bear to you." Othello next says the key words of the play: "And for that thou diest" (V,ii,46-48). Desdemona sees the twisted logic in his words, and, fair warrior to the end, corrects him. "That death's unnatural that kills for loving" she observes with amazing presence of mind, considering her situation. "Why gnaw you so your nether lip?" She is far past him now—mother, critic, reasonable kindergarten teacher, reminding him not to spit at his friends.

While he plays the role of judge and priest, a travesty of the masculine logos at work in the public world, Desdemona is at the other pole, the maternal eros on her bed, awaiting the underworld. Only when Othello says he has killed Cassio does Desdemona suddenly wake up, forget her sweet victim role, and say the honest, but exactly wrong thing: "Alas he is betrayed and I undone" (V,ii,92). The words sound like a confession, and Othello takes them as one. She breaks down completely, knowing that if he could kill Cassio, he could kill her. Up to now, the worst she thought could happen was divorce and banishment. Now she sees that the power she thought she had over this externalized animus was an illusion. He was never hers. She begs for time, always her security. Othello knows nothing of the world of time but lives only in the moment. He kills her while she's still talking and asking for time out. So Desdemona's last moments are a sharp clarification, a welcome to the real world where men are not gods.

Othello, as he is killing her, lies to himself, saying he is really being kind to kill her so fast and efficiently. Warriors know how to manage these peak moments. Meanwhile her female shadow, Emilia, is banging on the door. Othello begins to see the consequences of his act. The very sun and moon gape at what he has done. Now that he has put out Desdemona's light, his anima has moved to the stars. He cannot escape her gaze. Even when he blames his deed on the errors of the moon—mythically, woman and change—Desdemona speaks from beyond the grave. Here the play moves into myth, out of realism, out of Iago/Othello's sphere. Desdemona makes a threefold speech from the after-world, where the god of death, her chosen animus, has drawn her. She says she was murdered, was innocent, and in a moment that combines honesty with dishonesty in total, unreadable ambiguity, she says: nobody did this to me, except me. On one hand, she is still the fatuous child who loves her daddy/husband too much to see him as he is, but on the other, she is the spirit of forgiveness, having become transpersonal, acknowledging that perhaps she was in some way to blame, forgiving her murderer in the act of exonerating him.

We have seen enough of Desdemona in her last moments to be sure that she knows what's going on, that she has lost her power, and that Othello is not the god she thought he was. So it is a fair surmise that these words from beyond the grave are also beyond human game-playing, though they are literally a lie. Desdemona has paid with her life for her rebellion, her misreading of her mate, and for her attempts to take control of their relationship. She has become the figure of forgiveness, making it to maturation at the last minute. Jung says of such persons that, having accepted themselves, they are also able to become reconciled to adverse circumstances and events. The psychic reconciliation of Desdemona in death is complete. If she speaks in paradox, it is for the same reason that mystics speak in paradox; the truth does not polarize opposites, but unites them.

She leaves Emilia, a shadow awakening to full personality, to speak for her. Emilia has no idea that her husband was capable of such treachery. She is stupefied when she sees the truth, then cat-furious, first at Othello, then at Iago. "I'll make thee known," she screams at Othello. "Gull, Dolt. Unworthy of her." Iago comes on the scene all innocence, saying that he told Othello only "what he found himself was apt and true" (V,ii,209-10). He tries to make his wife go home, but Emilia will never again go home. The woman has now become the public side, the convicting presence in the world, while the murderous male has gone private, into silence and death. Othello is meanwhile waving his arms about, saying to the Venetians that this act may look bad, but he has good reasons for it. She sinned with Cassio a thousand times, and she gave Cassio Othello's handkerchief. Everybody's looking at everybody else as if Othello has suddenly turned into the Phantom of the Opera. Desdemona lies sprawled, dead on her wedding sheets, and this raving brute is worried about his image.

Except for grief over Emilia, whom Iago, true to his misogyny all the way, has called "filth" and run through with his sword, everyone's first thought is that Iago is the villain. It is certainly Othello's first thought, for he lunges at Iago. Strange that he does not kill him, for Othello is a warrior of great prowess. Yet he could be disarmed even by Montano, wounded severely just yesterday in the brawl. We must wonder if Othello has just as much trouble killing Iago as Hamlet has killing Claudius, and for the same reasons, because the other is his shadow, his other self. "As soon as that one dies, so will I," their thinking goes, and they are right.

The language of Othello as he comments on the murder is the fractured language of derangement: "Yes, 'tis Emilia—By and by. She's dead. . .Ha? No more moving" (V,II,92-102). Othello's earlier calm, poetic language was the language of his anima, a borrowed tongue. When he spoke it, he was not himself. Committing murder has brought him to the brink of consciousness, and he teeters on its verge. As Jung writes:

> A man who is unconscious of himself acts in a blind, instinctive way and is in addition fooled by all the illusions that arise when he sees everything that he is not conscious of in himself coming to meet him from outside as projections upon his neighbor. (*CW* 13,297/391)

And, of course, it is on Iago that Othello projects his guilt, as before he placed it on Desdemona. Iago, a step ahead of Othello, learns at last to shut up, projecting nothing. Language is no longer an option for him. As in Hamlet's terminal moments, "the rest is silence." Iago will not say another word. He admits no guilt and makes no apologies. Having destroyed Othello, he himself is already dead.

The dynamics of Othello's attempts at recognition are obvious. At first he was the smug, righteous avenger. Then he says stoically, reminding us of Hamlet in Act V, "Why should honor outlive honesty? Let it go all" (i.e., why should reputation outlive the reality of honor?). This observation is the nearest Othello gets to perception and moral clarity. He is not so much worried about murdering an innocent woman, but about how he will look in the eyes of the Venetians, who probably never thought much of his manners anyway. He reminds them how much he served the state. Poor Desdemona, "ill-starred wretch," had bad luck. The stars were against her. She'll probably curse him from heaven, damning him to hell. He still hasn't understood that she forgave him. Voices from beyond the grave are lost on some people. He anticipates and almost looks forward to his prospective tortures in hell. Even Rodrigo, in death, had the grace to call himself a villain, but Othello continues to blame Iago, and his own noble weakness, that of loving "not wisely but too well."

To the end, he thinks he loved Desdemona. Tell everybody how much I loved her, he begs, how miserably I was tricked, and while you're at it, say I served the state. Just as he pulls his dagger, he reminds the Venetians how he smote a traitorous Turk for assaulting a Venetian and betraying the state. Before he can give any thought to this damning analogy, he stabs himself. He dies upon a kiss, blaming his loss on fate, on Iago, projecting it everywhere but on himself. Then he splits-projects again, becoming executioner to the Turk. His last statement is only a fantastic story, not a perception. He kills himself and avoids admitting the truth.

The play begins and ends in darkness and uproar, framed by the ritual of marriage and the ritual of execution. Iago's world of goats and monkeys has conquered Othello's mythical world of open spaces, empty and heroic. Othello had attempted to combine the two worlds and failed. The public world, that of the masculine logos, is ruled by pride, the private one, of the maternal eros, by love. Ultimately, Othello cannot combine the two. One destroys the other, the bad angel firing the good one out. Sexuality, as Hillman says,

> is not only a creative gift we bestow on another, it is also a demonic force. Myths showing the cultivation of con-sciousness, such as the ones of...Gilgamesh...as well as primitive initiation rituals, indicate that the demonic aspect is to be tamed or avoided, sacrificed or withstood. We must *know* something about the inner darkness which contaminates our love. The shadow aspect of sexuality, especially in our long-repressed culture—must first become freed of its incestuous components, must first become connected with love and relatedness.[13]

Othello could not free himself from the terrible warrior, his shadow side, because he could not embrace his wife without fear.

The ego must not worship what is outside itself or project outside what is within. The wholeness of the Self depends on whether the ego can be forced to internalize the painful awareness of its shadow, thus transforming its shadow and transcending its small, limited self, as Desdemona is transformed by accepting her Othello-side as her own responsibility. The qualities are no longer so dark when they are brought into the light of day and one has the courage both to express them and hold them in check. From the psychological point of view, repression is not merely an evil, but is an opportunity for redemption, if one can acknowledge it, bringing it to consciousness.

Othello is the spider caught at the center of his own web. He is both the weaver (Iago) and the victim (his anima). Ultimately, as Hillman writes:

> after mid-life, providing that life up to its midpoint has seen a certain masculine development [as Othello's certainly had], the way is not the continuation along the same line. . .but rather the extension of the personality through its opposite [its femininity].[14]

A male can become the gentle man, the healer, the nourisher, the shaman, the round-bellied Buddha, the patient Christ. Instead, Othello chooses "marriage" to Iago and spiritual death—not death with transcendence, represented by Desdemona—just ordinary, ugly, meaningless death. Feeding the worms.

Othello marks the end of a series of plays beginning with *Hamlet* on the theme of "the sick Soul." Antony and Cleopatra begin in lust and fecklessness, but they end as mythical, sublime figures, dying into immortal love. With that play, tragedy begins to merge into miracle and myth, and in the world of *The Tempest*, the transformation is completed.

Chapter Three

The Tempest

Our own age is moving from written word to visual image. Shakespeare's was moving the other way, from the icons of the largely illiterate Middle Ages to the written word. Images are collective and impersonal, enjoyed in public, and based on simple, ideal forms accessible to the culture as a whole. The written word, on the other hand, is privately consumed, drawn from individual experience, and favors the complex and ambiguous over the simple and ideal. James Hillman distinguished between masculine sky (logos) and feminine earth (image) and wrote that over a thousand years ago soul and "images became subtly depotentiated" by theologians.[1] Drama links word and image, as do films and television today. *The Tempest*, with its pageant-masque and its central archetype of the emerging Self, is a particularly striking example of image and idea united in drama, and of the conflict between collective and individual man which marks the emergence of the modern era. In *The Tempest*, the soul, or our imaginative side, unites with spirit, the dazzling intellect. "Soul" deepens "events into experiences" and has a "special relation to death."[2] Ultimately, Prospero must balance otherworldly, intellectual images with those of his banished, repressed feminine soul, which speaks in images from nature.

Miranda and Ferdinand, in *The Tempest*, are female and male halves of the Self archetype, and their marriage represents the union of opposites Jung believed was necessary for the Self to emerge whole. They are characters in a drama with sociopolitical overtones, as well as ideal figures representing the two halves of the human psyche. In them, and in Prospero, whose emerging self they incarnate on the stage, Shakespeare acts out both the birth of the state and the birth of the individuated man. The low comedy of the clowns demonstrates the empirical level of reality in the play, while the noble lovers demonstrate the ideal. All, however, come together in Prospero's cave, indicating a marriage between empirical and ideal, of image and word.

The dominant philosophy of Shakespeare's time, Platonic idealism, was shaken by the rise of empiricism, yet held its ground. In

Shakespeare's plays, the archetypes act very much like the contents of imagination in the aesthetics of philosopher Pico Della Mirandola (d. 1494), a Platonist as Shakespeare himself probably was. Although Jung objected to Platonism's repression of the shadow and its consequent exaltation of a false freedom (*CW* 11,178/265), his archetypal theory resembles the Platonic ideas in the mind of God. Pico, for instance, held that the imagination is neither sensory nor rational, moral nor immoral, as Jung described the unconscious. Ariel, who represents imagination in *The Tempest,* served both the witch Sycorax and the noble Prospero. The object and what one intends to do with it determine whether the imagination is moral or immoral. Caliban's imagination can either dream of the island's music or it can lust after Miranda. The language of the imagination as of the unconscious is visual, not verbal. Its job is to present images to the intellect, which sorts through them to find the divine ideas.

The empiricist Francis Bacon (d. 1626) thought the noble Platonic forms, such as justice and love, had no reality in themselves. Such an attitude was characteristic of medieval nominalism. Jung writes of the triumph of nominalism over idealism: "This swing-over was accompanied. . .by the marked advance of empiricism" and the vanishing of the "primordial image" into *flatus vocis,* a mere breath (*CW* 11,i, pp. 75-75/149). The alchemist of Shakespeare's time resisted this reductionism, maintaining the medieval psychology of images as "basically aimed at soul-making."[3] Dr. John Dee, the alchemist and esoteric scholar banished by orthodox James I, may well have been the model for Prospero, making *The Tempest* a mystery play in which man's basic nature is transmuted into the pure gold of the divine self. If so, Prospero was the last of his kind, the last to exercise the transcendent function without suffering the fate of Faust. By the end of the Renaissance, feeling/sense had gone one way and thought the other. Plato's forms and their elegant order, imitated by the physical world, man, and human society, were down the cosmic drain. In their place we have the *Playboy* centerfold and *Popular Mechanics* to delight and instruct us.

Like Jung, Pico saw art and the spiritual in a single framework. What connected the two was reason. Jung wrote that man's turning away from instinct is what creates consciousness (*CW* 8,388/750), a concept Renaissance thinkers would have reduced to reason. Instinct is nature, for Jung, and seeks to perpetuate nature. It has its own unholy, delicious agenda, which becomes for romanticism the source of art. The Renaissance view of instinct is more Platonic than Jungian, resisting the contribution of untamed nature to the wholeness of the Self. Once the Caliban-like natural side had become thoroughly subdued by the reasonable, Prospero side, so Platonist thinking ran, harmony would prevail in both individual and state. Repression, not integration, was the way to go. For the Renaissance, reason subdued nature, as law and orderly hierarchical rule completed and perfected society. Reason was fast becoming to the individual what monarchy was to the rising state.

While Jung does not denigrate reason, he makes clear that it cannot exist without its opposite, the irrational:

> Consciousness should not be overrated...for experience provides too many incontrovertible proofs of the autonomy of unconscious compensatory processes for us to seek the origin of these antinomies only in the conscious mind. (*CW* 9ii,225-6/355)

Jung writes in *Psychological Aspects of the Mother Archetype* that we "should never forget that the world exists because its opposing forces are held in equilibrium" (*CW* 9i,94/174), as Prospero is with Caliban. Like any good Renaissance ruler, Prospero coexists uneasily with Caliban, representative of his inferior function, "feminine sensuality, an ever blessed wound" in the conscious personality through which the unconscious erupts and, with it, change.[4]

The static idealism of Platonic philosophy was under siege by 1600, and Shakespeare's dramatic tension, reflected in Prospero's touchiness, includes an awareness of the new empirical worldview, a diminished and distorted version of the old "feminine" sensuality and imagism. The coming of consciousness begins with internal conflict, as we see with Prospero. He doesn't wake up to material reality until he is thrown out of his kingdom by his Machiavellian younger brother and must make sense of his anger, desire for revenge, and duty to right the wrong of treason. He would have much preferred to stay in his library, dreaming his abstract, intellectual dreams. As Jung writes, "Nothing is so apt to challenge consciousness and awareness as being at war with oneself" (*CW* 11,10/639). The conflict is compounded by the naive, conservative urge to view such self-consciousness as the primordial sin of breaking up original unity. Metaphorically, in *The Tempest*, divided state and divided hero are the same. They act out the drama of Shakespeare's own time, when the thousand-year medieval monolith of Platonic idealism was challenged by empirical scientists, merchants, and individualists. When Prospero made the shift from library to liberation, from books to practical statesmanship, he seized Promethean lightning with both hands. Once he had gone to sea, that is, faced death, he could not go home again as the same man. For the deeper drama being acted out in *The Tempest* is that of an exile coming home to consummate a marriage of opposites.

The explorer of Shakespeare's time was a metaphor of the interior voyager in strange seas of thought. What he found in his explorations was alien and primitive, a challenge to his own unrecognized shadow. The new mythology of colonial discovery pitted the primitive world against the European civilized world of mind, as we have seen in *Othello*. This myth of the New World was Shakespeare's source for *The Tempest*, along with the hermeticism and esoteric initiation rites of both the classical and the Christian past. The savage west was the new labyrinth and Caliban was the minotaur at the center of the maze,[5] for in Shakespeare's time, the inhabitants of the New World were thought hardly human, except by Montaigne, who in Florio's translation may have influenced Shakespeare's humanizing of Caliban. New World savages were considered monsters of sensuality, threats to the religion of reason evolving in Renaissance Europe. They were rapists, irredeemably natural, requiring the knout and the boot to control them, like women and blacks.

Savages, along with empiricists and cynics like Iago or Antonio, turn up with increasing frequency in Shakespeare. The play *Troilus and Cressida* is exclusively populated by hustlers and cynics representing a whole spectrum of human savagery. *The Tempest* has its share of "new men," with no morals, no values, and no faith. When Stephano and Antonio first see Caliban, they think about how much they could make by selling him, indifferent to traditional beliefs in Platonic archetypes and lawful order. Each is morally the half-man that Caliban is physically.

The lower classes in *The Tempest* reenact the treason of their betters; Caliban is entrained in Stephano's will-to-power as Sebastian is in Antonio's. Caliban is a cut above the two degenerate servants, for he is a primitive with the capacity for childlike devotion. He is also capable of poetry, while his new masters speak in prose. His poetry is heavy with consonants, with snarls, mutterings, and hissings: "But they'll nor pinch/Fright me with urchin-shows, pitch me i' the mire... adders, who with cloven tongues/Do hiss me into madness" (II,ii,5-14). His is the language of the senses, graphic, vivid, and prone to the same mistakes that the senses are, in the Renaissance view. When he sees Trinculo, he thinks him a spirit; when he sees Stephano and drinks from his sherry bottle, he thinks Stephano a god. As Prospero gave Caliban his poetry, so Stephano gives him another, lesser language. Caliban finds a bogus freedom in servitude to these two drunks, offering them what he offered Prospero—access to the natural secrets of the island. In addition, he offers what is not his to give, rule of the isle and marriage to Miranda. His new status as a "free man" has addled what slight wits he had. Shakespeare's view of the common man's capacity for self-determination is a dim one, as we see by these three. If the other people on this island be brained like us, says Trinculo, "the state totters" (III,ii,5-6). He's right. The state of Naples is tottering on the brink of treason, even as Prospero's own mind totters on the brink of obsession with revenge.

The moral freakishness of a Caliban or Stephano is a form of Jung's ego-inflation, which we see frequently in *The Tempest*, even in the character of the sublime Prospero. When the "ego is assimilated by the self," it is a "psychic catastrophe," Jung writes in *CW* 9ii,24/45. "If, therefore," he continues, "the ego falls for any length of time under the control of an unconscious factor, its adaptation is disturbed and the way opened for all sort of accidents." Such an accident occurs when the idea of wholeness–the very basis of a matured self--remains unconscious, resulting in an inflated ego and often in a Hitlerian frenzy, as in the case of the murderous traitor, Antonio, Prospero's brother. Even Prospero is tempted to be a cruel, vengeful autocrat. He skirts the line between being swallowed by his ego and overcoming it, the line between tragedy and transcendence.

Jung might be writing of Prospero's ultimate triumph over ego-inflation when he notes that "it is of the greatest importance that the ego should be anchored in the world of consciousness and that consciousness should be reinforced by a very precise adaptation." Such adaptation depends on moral discipline, as in cultivation of the virtues which include patience and humility (not Prospero's strong suit) and "observation of unconscious symptoms as they erupt" (*CW* 9ii,24-25/46). The risk of ego-inflation was accompanied on the positive side by the growth of individual consciousness and moral responsibility for one's own interior life.

Almost until the end of the play, Prospero proudly separates himself from the people around him, whom he treats as his inferiors. Back in Milan, he had been a typical professor, living in his head, dissociating his mind from his body, divorcing concept from experience. His wife probably lived on Valium and soap operas, waiting for him to come out of his library. He may have doubted that Miranda was his child because he couldn't remember begetting her. In any case, he has recreated her out of his own head, and in his own image, as Zeus gave birth to Athena, pure, virginal, and disembodied.

When all the monsters and villains of ordinary mortal life swarm onto the island, Prospero must at last confront the beast of his own ego and its fears, no longer repressing and projecting them. He must differentiate and clarify his own unconscious depths, bringing them to consciousness and confronting the mortality they represent. Toward the end of the play, Prospero has accepted the impending death of his aged body. He must also accept and acknowledge emotion and moral weakness as part of himself, as he does when he admits to loss of temper at the disruption of his marriage masque. Once the feminine has been accepted, it loses its negative charge and changes from a Sycorax to a Miranda.[6] Ultimately, he not only makes no effort to hold onto his magic powers, but voluntarily gives them up. Before his psyche can be unified in the last phases of spiritual initiation, the fragments must be acknowledged and humbly gathered together.

In the beginning, Prospero is a thoroughly compartmentalized modern man. He has Miranda as his merciful heart, Ariel to handle his prefrontal lobes, and Caliban to "haul the logs," that is, to express his passion, his bestial side, and that of all men. Norman Holland points out that wood was originally spelled "wode," meaning mad or animal-like. In Shakespeare, reference to wood or wooden connotes brutishness. The "woodman" suggests a hunter of women and enslavement to the passions. Caliban is a woodman forced to sublimate his passion for Miranda into carrying logs. His opposite number is Ferdinand, who obediently accepts his logs, his passionate side, knowing that freedom has its limits, as does patriarchal power. Fathers can die, a truth Ferdinand, unlike Hamlet, freely accepts. Prospero says he will manacle Ferdinand's head to his feet, symbolically linking above to below. Ferdinand is to eat acorn husks and roots, the food of pigs, animals sacred to the Great Mother.[7] He is the young king, a "divine *puer*," born of the Great Mother from the sea. He is the other half of the *senex*, old Prospero, who begins the play exhibiting "melancholy, anxiety, sadism, and paranoia," a man created in the image of a wifeless, remote "senex god," the God of our culture.[8] Through Miranda, both *puer* and *senex* are made whole and human.

Miranda's fiercely guarded chastity is an example of virtue as the balance between soul and body, freedom and obedience to social restraints. Chaste marriage is the metaphor of harmony and justice in society. In the Act IV masque, Ceres-Demeter promises fertility if the lovers behave themselves, obeying the just restrictions of the father. Justice and plenty in the realm depend on virtue of the rulers, as King

James I wrote in his *Basilikon Doron*. If the ruler is lecherous, like Claudius, the kingdom will decay, a connection reminiscent of that figure from Arthurian myth, the wounded Fisher King and his barren country. Chastity and justice, linked together in the Renaissance, were not the mere abstractions they are today. Justice to us means that if I hang your hostage, you have a right to hang mine. The Renaissance idea of justice was human action directed toward a rightful end. Both chastity and justice were part of government, concerns of the state and of the father, representative of God and state in the family.

To represent God properly, Prospero must first transcend his Caliban-like lower nature. For most of the play, he's concentrating on his obsession with revenge, like Hamlet and Othello. Because he's too old to be subservient to lust, he's past the more infantile and adolescent self-identifications with outward forms. But his ego is giving him a hard time. The main trouble is the projections he's so expert at creating. Just as he projects his irrational, passionate unconscious onto Caliban, he projects his failure as a ruler onto Antonio. Both Caliban and Antonio are shadow figures, belonging half to Prospero's personal unconscious and half to the collective one. The shadow's "effect on the personality as a whole lies in compensating the ego," preventing a "dissociation of the personality," that typically occurs when the ego takes over at the expense of a man's heart.[9] Antonio was the part of Prospero that wanted to rule, and such a desire had its positive side—taking responsibility in the material world, which Prospero had tried to evade.

Although for Miranda's sake, Prospero puts the best face he can on Antonio's corporate takeover, the picture we get in Act I is clear. For a long time, Prospero had sat in his library, not caring whether or not Milan was threatened by toxic wastes. He was busy turning into a white magician, losing his dukedom by repressing his shadow side and letting others embody it for him. Antonio had been running Milan all this time, and even Prospero doesn't say he was doing a bad job. One day Antonio decided he wanted the name of duke along with the work, in his own way trying to unify the fragments and become whole. So he packed Prospero and his baby daughter into a dinghy and pushed them out to sea, headed nowhere. Prospero said Antonio didn't kill them only because he would have been afraid of the people, who bore their duke a great love. How would he know, locked up in the library as he was? The people had probably forgotten all about him. If they hadn't, Antonio would hardly have dared to get rid of duke and daughter as he did. The next day, Antonio marched into Milan's Pentagon like Alexander Haig and proclaimed himself in charge. It didn't hurt him with the generals that he had the support of King Alonso of Naples during the coup. What is especially important about this early part of Prospero's life is that he is "thrown" into the real world, away from his womblike study, his Eden, and must go through the same initiation process as others in the play before he returns home.

Prospero started his splitting of father and mother figures—his fragmentation of himself—even before leaving Milan. He remembers Gonzalo as the sweet old father who put books in the boat and Alonso as the evil king who betrayed him. The two always appear together throughout the play, perhaps prefiguring Prospero's attempts at unifying the fragments of himself. Ultimately Alonso is forgiven, healing the split. Hamlet was unable to reconcile the good and bad fathers, Claudius and old Hamlet; thus he was condemned to fall between them. For we cannot integrate only one side, repressing the other, as Othello found out. He needed both Iago and Cassio in order to live. Prospero, on the other hand, is establishing his center, his balance point, throughout the play. Jung focused on the total personality, drawing a line between conscious and unconscious, and keeping a foot in each, establishing a solid foundation for the personality. The conflict between mighty opposites must strain the psyche to the breaking point. Only then, Jung writes, can the grace of marriage fall on persona and shadow, joining them, blending conscious and unconscious.[10] Throughout most of Prospero's life the two are separate and the self remains an ideal to be sought. Not in the grubby purgatory of Milan but in the terrestrial paradise of the island is the ideal ultimately realized.

The archetype of the Self, in alchemy, was represented by the sun, the egg yolk, or the point. It is the gold into which the alchemists tried to turn base metals. Jung cites from a Gnostic precursor of the alchemists: "This Man is a single Monad, uncompounded (and) indivisible…loving and at peace with all things (yet) warring with all things and at war with itself in all things…showing forth all things and giving birth to all things."[11] The emblem of this Man is the point. It is both God and man, and is the principle from which the soul proceeds and to which it returns. This pearl of great price, Jung writes, represents "an assimilation and integration of Christ into the human psyche" (*CW* 9ii,221/346). Prospero tries to turn the dross of human nature into gold, and succeeds only in transforming himself.

As Shakespeare matured, the archetype of the Self, freed of ego desires and appetites, grew more significant in his plays. The projections became more sharp and vicious. Antonio, in *The Tempest,* is far more evil than Claudius, who after all had his little winning ways.

Antonio is a rat and nothing but a rat. Gonzalo is a sweet, witless old man, and Stephano a drunken fool. They might as well be wearing masks. They might as well be walking archetypes without personality or ego. They are not real and not intended to be real. They might be mere figments of Prospero's imagination, dreamed by him, created like snakeskins and shed when outgrown.

The personae of the characters become progressively less clear in the late plays, while the anima and the archetype of the Self become more so. Jung notes that just as the anima/animus syzygy (pair of opposites) is more complex than the shadow, so the archetype of wholeness is higher than the syzygy. It is represented by the divine child (CW 9ii,59/31). In *The Tempest*, the feminine form of that child is Miranda, who also embodies the highest qualities of the anima. Miranda picks up where Desdemona and Cleopatra leave off—rebellious, merciful, heading for psychic marriage, for Psyche's divine union with Eros, no matter what the men in her life want or say they want. None of these females has to cope with the Terrible Mother; they have assimilated her. They no longer have the problems of the female ego, threatened by relatedness, preferring beauty to knowledge, fearing the underworld. Having assimilated masculine order, they have advanced beyond the men and initiate the men into maturation. Such women are led by the divine child, either within themselves or objectively represented outside themselves. Ferdinand is both animus and child archetype, appearing as both Miranda's future husband and the beautiful youth who will complete her passage into wholeness.

Perhaps the first sign of a mature connection between male and female comes in the middle of *Antony and Cleopatra*, as if Shakespeare had been suddenly knocked off his donkey on the way to Damascus. Cleopatra had begun the play as a sluttish, shrewd opportunist. She ends it as a goddess, a woman who sees beyond the world of power and dreams of more than shopping in the Alexandria mall. Antony begins as a lustful glutton, a party boy, a Hefner, and ends like Tristan, convulsed in a love-death, a union with his feminine opposite that is much more *dulcis et utile* than living by the rules, as does that dull, self-righteous yuppie, Octavius.

The wife figures in Shakespeare's plays don't make it to the anima stage, except possibly Hermione, in *The Winter's Tale*, written just before *The Tempest*. In that play, devoted to the creative power of women, the wife is killed off early and returns to forgive her murderous, jealous, Othello-like husband at the end. As in so many of Shakespeare's later plays, the daughter figure is the one who carries the power of the anima.

Perdita, in *The Winter's Tale*, is a Persephone who reunites angry men, brings back the spring, and even causes her mother to return to the living. Paulina, the crone who unites the daughter with her middle-aged mother, is the catalyst for the whole play's action, while the men react helplessly, thrashing around in the unfamiliar sea of emotion into which their inner and outer women have dumped them. Leontes, the erring king, is an unconscious Prospero, jealous, tyrannical, minded to incest and perhaps to juvenile homosexuality, intent on power and insistent on subservience in all his inferiors. The play sprawls over sixteen years and several countries, while the characters attain no individuality and slight self-knowledge. Wherever Shakespeare was in his own life when he wrote *The Winter's Tale*, he wasn't at his dramatic best.

Miranda, like other late heroines of Shakespeare, serves her man, educates her father in mercy, and retains her virginal innocence till the end, seeing the world as brave and new, even though it has Antonios in it. The Terrible Mother has no part in her. Nor does the vengeful, accusatory Dido, who, like other rejected, ghostly females, stalks the burial ground of Greek myth and tragedy, the ground of the unconscious. Sycorax, who once ruled the island, dies before the play begins, as does Miranda's mother. Prospero says little about his wife, except those mysterious words indicating that probably she was virtuous, that probably Miranda is his child. From the beginning of *The Tempest*, we have a sense that the myth being enacted is the consolidation of patriarchal power, the power of reason, of mind, over the Dionysiac emotion of the witch-female, the hounder of infant-men to toilet seats, baths, and homework.

Prospero splits the mother image as he does the father's. On one hand, we hear him briefly remember Miranda's mother and his motherland, Milan. On the other, we have the island of Sycorax, the witch-mother. Once the island had languished in unconsciousness, without language, without morality, under the matriarch, the mother of half-men. Mythically, Prospero is describing the transition from the mother goddess's neolithic village to the city-states of the philosopher kings, patriarchs like himself, who create order and teach the half-men to talk, diversify their labor, and create civilization. Sycorax, the witch-mother, locks up Ariel, the imaginative principle, inside a tree; Prospero, the white magician, the father-healer, lets him out.

The tree or plant represents the unconscious state, the unawakened personality, Jung writes in *The Spirit Mercurius*. In the Osiris myth, the tree trunk or *djed* pillar was a symbol of immortality, of our longing for an integrated, permanent soul.[12] Enclosed in the tree trunk, the son goes through various larval stages in his psychic development. The Osiris myth shows the soul still in the dark womb, unconscious, unable to leave the mother's power, asleep in protective darkness, dreaming of freedom, dreaming of consciousness. Freeing Ariel from the tree trunk is mythologically freeing the son from the mother, and the beginning of his ascent into individuation. Both Ariel and Miranda are anima figures for Prospero, who turns to them alternately, not at the same time. They never see or speak to each other, but Prospero integrates them both into himself by the end, as he sets them free. Once he has integrated his anima, he no longer needs these external representations of her and can stand alone.

The mother image is split between Sycorax, the mother of monsters, and Miranda, the potential mother of kings. Under Sycorax, the island had languished in unconsciousness, without language, without morality. Miranda, of course, was never under the sway of Sycorax. She survives a possible fall into sin with Ferdinand and becomes a new Eve, mother of a new race. The mother-spirit of the island is long gone, and only her animal son is left to remind us of her and her ancient rule. We hear only faint echoes of the matriarchy that so awkwardly said its piece in *Winter's Tale*. Now the only issue that matters is a man's peace, his ability to subdue his passion and be merciful.

Prospero has internalized the Terrible Mother issue into a conflict between his angry passion to control others and his reasonable will to achieve justice, express forgiveness, and die a simple soul, without magic or illusion. We see the conflict during Prospero's first speech, for Shakespeare's habit is to show us from the beginning some hint of what drives his main characters.[13] Prospero irritably demands Miranda's attention and sympathy as he talks about his administrative failures. Despite this tendency to peevishness, he has raised Miranda to be forthright and honest. Maybe too much so for her own good, he worries, when Ferdinand shows up. Once before he let a younger person take over his rightful place as ruler, and he's nervous now that Miranda has developed a mind of her own.

When Prospero tells innocent Miranda about his own fall from grace, early in Act I, he is telling the story of his failure, his King Lear phase, when he let others decide for him. Miranda, listening dutifully to him, can hardly stay awake. Until Ferdinand, her animus-come-to-life appears, she's sleepwalking, as much a faceless creature of her father's as Ariel is. She is unconscious because she is still a virgin, virginity being a metaphor of the soul's purity and simplicity before its violation by experience, before it is dragged down to the underworld by the rapist/husband, the masculine force that unites the female with her own body, her soul, her Self. Ophelia could only experience this unity by suicide, by drowning herself when she had lost both lover and father. Once her two animus figures were gone, she did not exist, having never built a self. Ophelia was the unconscious, waiting to come out of the closet. Nobody opened the door, and she was too weak to open it herself, as Miranda does.

Miranda is willing, even eager, for the unconscious in her to rise and come out carrying logs. She makes outrageous offers of service, of unconditional love. Polonius told Ophelia how to be a proper court lady, and she followed his advice to an early grave; Prospero tells Miranda how to be herself, and she obliges him by disobedience. If Hamlet had fallen in love with Miranda instead of Ophelia, he would have thrown Claudius off the ramparts before Act II. But unlike Ferdinand, he would not risk separation from the Terrible Mother, from the image he had formed of himself as entwined with her. He would not love, because he hated himself for loving the wrong person—Gertrude, the Sycorax of Elsinore. Nor could Othello give up his mother and her handkerchief in order to love and trust Desdemona. To take innocence from a woman, to unite with her, for such a man as Othello, was to become womanly, to make himself a poor eunuch, a man whose sword has been surrendered to the domestic order and the woman.

Prospero begins as a jealous Brabantio and ends by releasing his daughter to another man. In letting Miranda be herself, in releasing her from his anxious manipulations, Prospero ironically becomes himself, transformed through her. He begins by scolding and brutalizing Ferdinand and ends by marrying the young prince to Miranda. Persephone has made a successful comeback; Psyche has mothered Joy, a divine Self, in defiance of the Terrible Mother, and she wins the hero's soul away from mother, away from the prescriptions of a society which would rob him of himself. Prospero is now allowed to die, a free man, in the arms of his own soul. The same theme of death and rebirth is suggested in the marriage of Claribel (meaning bright, beautiful) to the African king, which happened before the play begins. She is a successful Desdemona, a European who has achieved union with her dark African opposite. As in *Antony and Cleopatra*, East and West have mythically come together. Though cynical Sebastian tries to degrade this happy integration of opposites,[14] it prefigures the integration that Prospero is building in himself.

Prospero is not merely a ruler who wants vengeance like Hamlet and Othello, or power for its own sake. Prospero's abilities transcend the conscious intellect and princely power. He is the wise old man of folk legends and dreams, the Obi Wan Kenobi who is the source of strength when technology and reason fail. Like a shaman, Prospero is the healer/killer, the one who administers poison so that the patient may live. He echoes the tradition of the old British kingship, in which the king has two bodies, the personal and the royal. In the latter form, the king is able like the Savior to heal with a touch.[15] A source of both good and evil, he takes the sick person through denial to affirmation, through suffering to heaven, and he does his work in a magical dream state.

Because he forces material from the unconscious to the conscious mind, first wounding in order to cure, Prospero can be seen as a daemon, a source of sin. More Greek than romantic or modern, Prospero is both dark daemon and bright god. Like Hades, he is most at home in darkness. Like Apollo in his chariot, he drives two horses: Caliban, the sluggish, unwilling one, and Ariel, the fiery and excitable one.[16] The task challenging Prospero is not only to reorder the external world, but to learn how to balance and control the inner world. To do so, he must undergo an initiation rite that begins in his near-death at sea and is only completed by the end of the play.

Prospero is at once Orpheus the musician, Asclepius the healer, and Prometheus, the bringer of conscious fire, the "eternal artist rejected by the society his art redeems."[17] He is also a failed ruler, a bitchy old man, and loser in love, since his daughter opts for her chosen animus and for that brave new world, the future, in which her old father has no part. Prospero is not only himself, but a trinity. The shadows "are themselves on the stage...[and] also represent the unacknowledged portion of the hero's personality," what Jung calls the "repressed tendencies," the shadow which, though not necessarily evil, is "somewhat inferior, primitive, unadapted, and awkward." This shadow may contain qualities "which would ...vitalize and embellish human existence (*CW* 9i,78/134). That is, a Caliban, though he must be kept on a short leash, would be the poet that Antonio could not be and the lover Prospero had never been. Caliban is the shadow that Prospero has to face, that Jung says all of us must face before we can experience individuation.

The figure in Shakespeare who comes nearest to being a priest and a saint, Prospero is what Hamlet would have been had Hamlet lived and not become indifferent to his life, his purpose blunted. Like Hamlet, Prospero attempts to achieve individuation through intellect alone, but Miranda and Ariel prevent him from drying up in his rationality. The fire Prospero/Prometheus steals from heaven could just as well be from hell, for it can burn as well as empower. Ariel and Caliban are both part of the world as it is, part of Prospero. He ultimately frees them as he frees himself, not by magic but by prayer, not by public justice but by private compassion. He goes through a process of metamorphosis, like everyone else in the play. Words like "melt" and "dissolve" characterize the last act that is a dream, a world that is an evanescent dance of atoms. Change is all that we can be sure of, in the world of *The Tempest*. Prospero is trying to change himself into a man who can function authentically in this world, who can integrate his fragmented self.

We tend to equate human completeness with adaptability, adjustment to the social world, conformity to collective expectations. The "mana-personality" like Prospero's is nonconformist,[18] the enemy of mass culture. Prospero's spiritual exile serves a purpose—self-realization, a turning away from the court, with its rules and posturing. As his power recedes, his self-knowledge increases. He becomes a metaphor of human transcendence over the unconscious, of awareness over mere sense perception. Like Prometheus, he has brought down fire from heaven for the use of men, and he has suffered for his trouble. The spirit aches when it must contract to fit temporal forms, and Prospero's cramps hurt as much as Caliban's.

Prospero's island is caught between chaotic storms and music, between the opposition of individualism (ego) and the collective world of the unconscious represented by tradition. Only in Shakespeare's last four plays is the marriage between tempest and music consummated. The archetype of the musician-healer officiates at this marriage, allowing the integration of soul and body, of masculine and feminine, to take place. Prospero thus represents the archetype of the healer, though he must first be joined with Miranda, the heart of mercy. The end of suffering is harmony between the music and the hearer. Ophelia heard in Hamlet's words a discord; Othello disliked music; Caliban heard in the island's twanging sounds a heavenly song. With the playing of music and the spectacle of masques, the contents of the unconscious safely come up, are observed, and are assimilated.

The storm that rages around the island at the beginning of the play is an obvious metaphor of the conflict within Prospero himself. The tempest dominates and orders the action. Even the political discord of his last days in Milan is rerun when the storm hits: the ruler of the ship, the Boatswain, getting an argument from his passengers, who refuse to go below and thus "assist the storm." "You don't like the way we're handling the boat?" he says in effect to Antonio, who is calling him a whore's son. "Then shut up and help." The villainous Antonio says he's "out of patience" with this storm, a situation which follows him around. He cannot bear a reality that ignores him and his inflated ego. This brief glimpse of man in danger of death is metaphorically one of his terror at the unknown, the loss of his control and his ego, the breaking up of all his fragile attempts at order. Prospero causes this storm, i.e., he is willing to bring up all the contents of his unconscious at once, because he is ready to face his daemons and to lift the people around him to the next stage of self-realization.

As Prospero rose reborn from the sea, so must all the others in the play. In him, consciousness rises from the sea of the unconscious, as happens mythically during baptism, and in Avalon, the "Isles of the Blest," Elysium, and the river Styx.[19] For ancient and medieval philosophers the universe was composed of four main spheres through which the soul passes in its progress to God: the realm of earth (mortal life), water (the dead), air, and aether. Jung writes in *Aion* of the four elements which together form the *spiritus mundi*, the soul of the earth, and the Self, that singular point of divine energy within each human being (*CW* 9ii,250-1/394-5). Of the elements, fire and air are too mysterious to know anything about except by analogy, assuming that the next world is reliably represented by this one. These parallels are the basis of mythological traditions and find their way into the highest forms of art.[20] *The Tempest* is one such form.

The Tempest is more than a collection of mythic themes embodying Elizabethan sociopolitical concerns. It is a rite of initiation into wholeness, as much a sacred mystery play as a secular drama. Jung believed that Christian images and rituals did not spring full-blown into the Western mind during the first century A.D. Its forms were borrowed from paganism, as its cathedrals were built on the ruins of pagan temples: "We are inevitably stamped as Christians; but we are also stamped by that which existed before Christianity."[21] Christian symbols are, for Jung, also symbols that represent the kingdom of God, psychic wholeness, the "assimilation and integration of Christ into the human psyche" (*CW* 9ii,221/346). Thus, *The Tempest* can be read as a story going back into the rituals of European prehistory, of the soul's rise from the mud of earth into the bright realm of spirit. In fact, if we do not read it as a dramatization of primitive, pagan, and Christian initiation rituals, a lot of loose ends are left hanging. The whole thing otherwise seems like a labored, two-dimensional, overly obvious allegory of good overcoming evil. Except for some funny drunk scenes, the realist critic finds little to amuse him, and except for Prospero's relationship with his daughter, the Freudian critic finds little to work on. A Jungian reader, on the other hand, finds a rich mine, with more mythic gold than a modern audience has the mythological background to dig out, unless we research the esoteric lore which was as familiar to Shakespeare's time as the lives of sports heroes and rock stars are to our own. The work of art closest to it is Mozart's *The Magic Flute*, with its roots deep in Masonic ritual, and which, like Shakespeare's last play, combines comic, mythic, and mystical themes in a secular version of the medieval mystery play.

No sources for *The Tempest* exist except in classical mythology, accounts of the Eleusinian mysteries, and Christian mystical tradition. Shakespeare himself grew up on medieval mystery plays, which were commonly performed in his neighborhood throughout his youth. When the shift to masques, miracles, and myth came over the Elizabethan theater in the early 1600s, Shakespeare did not have far to look for a subject. In England and on the continent, the alchemists and Platonists were resurrecting the ancient beliefs in esoteric rituals and wisdom. It was a strategic moment for the rise of these long-underground spiritual forms. Medieval Catholicism was losing its monolithic character and its power to enforce a literal belief in the events of the Gospel. Protestantism, though cursed with its own rigidities, offered individuals the opportunity to read and interpret Scripture on the basis of individual conscience. Renaissance scholarship had spread wide knowledge of Greek texts, with their references to the mystery religions of the pre-Christian era.

The time was ripe for a fusion of Gnostic wisdom, pagan ritual, and Christian esotericism. Dante had shown the way, having been guided by Virgil through Hell, and by Beatrice, a Mary/Sophia figure, through the terrestrial paradise. Shakespeare broadened the road, including more than biblical and Roman classical references and secularizing the whole scene. He wrote in accordance with Elizabethan theatrical taste and a new worldview enriched by exploration on continents only recently known and by a cosmos only recently discovered to be vast, changing, and not centered on the earth. *The Tempest* is a mystery play for moderns, a drama that draws together Christian, pagan, and contemporary philosophic beliefs on government, self-knowledge, ethics, and religion.

The play is a "dramatic representation of the Mystery of Redemption, conceived as a psychological experience and expressed in mythological form."[22] Redemption in *The Tempest* is the rise of man from the mire of earthly desires, in which he has wallowed since the fall, as well as his wanderings through ordeals and painful lessons in virtue. When he wakes up, he accepts the conditions of his initiation and enters, with the help of a feminine figure or spirit guide, into Elysium, the Christian heaven, or the mystical bliss of enlightenment, depending on the mythic form you choose.

Stephano and Trinculo enact the fall of man, the court party moves through the Lesser Initiation of the Eleusinian mysteries, and Ferdinand completes the Greater Initiation, ending in the paradise of marriage to Miranda and kingship. The Lesser Initiation is a purgatory of frustrating ordeals, wanderings through a dark labyrinth, while the senses are tempted and disciplined. Lucian gave these words to a character lost in a dark maze: "You have been through the Eleusinian mysteries. Tell me now, do you not think this is very like them?"[23] Perhaps because Ferdinand has few sins to expiate, his initiatory wandering in darkness is brief. He quickly finds Miranda and paradise then enters the Greater Initiation. The same island can be purgatory or paradise, according to your psychological state. The Greater Initiation takes the soul from the element of air into fiery aether. A symbolic death to the sense world occurs as the soul moves from reason to intuition.

To each person on it, the island is different, for it is an imaginative construct, not a real, physical place. Each character sees the island from his own point of view. When Caliban describes to drunken Stephano the twanging sounds of invisible instruments played by the island's spirits:

Be not afeard. The isle is full of noises,
Sounds and sweet airs that give delight and hurt not.
Sometimes a thousand twangling instruments
Will hum about mine ears...(III,ii,143)

Stephano retorts from his crass, commercial soul, "I shall get my music for nothing." In the eyes of the common, grasping "new men," like Stephano and Antonio, the island is nothing but a place to ravish, exploit, own. The psyche of colonial Europe was born in this period, among such men. To the aristocratic Ferdinand, however, the island is a prison in which he would be happy to see Miranda through the bars (I,ii,600-605). Caliban sees the island as the source of pignuts, the land where he should rightfully rule. Ferdinand, by Act IV, sees it as a paradise in which he would gladly stay, to be ruled by such a father as Prospero.

From the beginning, the island has a shimmering unreality about it. The rules of the logical mainland are not in effect here.[24] When people swim to shore, their clothes are not even wet and, in fact, look better than before. Of course, nobody at the Globe theater wanted to ruin a lot of good costumes, but the point is that the sea-change is an improvement. A moral improvement is also underway. The sinners are led by harpies into the wilderness and offered dinner, only to have it snatched away. Music comes and goes while spirits chase Alonso's party, reminding the men of their lost connection between conscience and conduct. Shakespeare often links playing and listening to psychic processes. If you hear sweet music, your savagery will be charmed into a sweetness to match. The music entrains you to the cosmic harmonies of the crystalline spheres; it inspires you to unify the fragments of your broken personality. A potential miracle of healing is metaphorically signified by the curative effect of music on the discordant mind, giving it the model of patience and order in the midst of chaotic pain. The musical island, where all nature is in balance and harmony, is the world of childhood, the unconscious on the verge of consciousness. When Caliban describes his earlier life on the island, his time of innocence, he speaks fondly, in poetry whose harsh consonants echo his brutish nature, as well as his animal innocence: "Let me bring thee where crabs grow/And I with my long nails will dig thee pignuts" (II,ii,163-4). Before he lost Father Prospero's love by attacking Miranda, Caliban loved him and learned from him how to name the stars. He was allowed to share the family cave, until his adolescent testosterone surged, and he attempted to people the isle with Calibans, that is, wanted to usurp the kingdom and become what Prospero was. Stephano tries to do the same thing, unaware that to rule you must have something more than a butt of sack and a big mouth.

The island is also an interior landscape, full of dangerous sinkholes as well as heavenly music. The hero must overcome his tendency to fall into old patterns, such as courtly, inappropriate behavior with the innocent Miranda. He must also give up his reliance on physical power, as when Ferdinand vainly attempts to threaten Prospero with a sword. To surrender and not act is what he must learn. Miranda simply appears to Ferdinand. He doesn't have to do any more than swim to the island and start walking around, following Ariel's music. His imagination offers him Miranda and assigns her a divine meaning in his life. Stephano and Antonio, however, lunge around the island trying to conquer it. Unlike Ferdinand, they are frustrated and gain nothing, neither materially nor in the way of self-knowledge. They are sunk in filthy bogs. For them, the island is a rerun of life in the outside world: savage and ugly. No Miranda appears to them; they get only harpies. The point is that you get what your imagination is capable of conceiving, based on your motivation, your training, and the capacity of your intellect to organize images into wholesome, useful forms. A benevolent anima figure like Miranda does not propose to you unless you are prepared by grace and nobility of character to receive her.

Music draws Ferdinand to Miranda and in general leads all the visitors into a dream state, into sleep or trance on this Fantasy Island where nothing is what it seems. Back in Milan, Prospero himself was in a trance, bemused by his books. Now, on the island, he puts others into trance states in order to educate them. In each person, the real motives emerge as he sinks into his own unconscious and experiences suffering, getting a good look at his motives and the extent of his bonds with others. The island is a kind of psychic ecosystem in which we are all caught. In their trance states, the men all experience not being their own (V,i,249-50), not being in control of their reason, not being sure of anything. They are back in the world of childhood, the mysterious world where adults were in charge of the physical arrangements and the children in charge of make-believe. In this case, Prospero controls both, bringing up a motley family.

His educational strategy must be adapted to the limitations of his students, who range from sinning Adam to redeemed souls. The Fall of Man takes place before the play begins, but it is reenacted by the misadventures of the childish Stephano and Trinculo. In the primitive time before Prospero came to the island, a pregnant witch had settled there. Sycorax (*sy*, meaning pig, and *corax*, meaning curved, or bent out of [moral] shape) has affinities to Hecate, who is represented as having a boar's head. Osiris is pictured as spearing a boar, an animal which in patriarchal mythology is synonymous with evil. Sycorax controlled moon and tides, and Caliban is her son by the devil Setebos, a Patagonian devil-god known to Elizabethan England through Eden's *History of Travayle in the West and East Indies* (1577). The name of the island's god may also be related to the Egyptian "Seteb," meaning what is hostile or evil, and related to the murderous god Set. Caliban's physical qualities betray his origin; he looks and stinks like a fish. Joseph Campbell remarks on the frequency of fish-men in the mystery rituals of the Near East. In the Orphic mysteries, the Lord of the Abyss is "enthroned upon a scaly sea-beast, a sort of modified crocodile."[25] This divinity with his hammer was both creator and destroyer of the illusion that is the world. Life emerges from its watery abyss and returns to it in death. Both Caliban and his mother are associated with water, the element of desire, femininity, wantonness—the place where hateful, dangerous mythological monsters lie in wait for travelers.

Sycorax is the Whore of Babylon, the Kali, the destructive feminine bitch, while Miranda is her polarized opposite, the Virgin/Wisdom figure. In *The Winter's Tale*, Shakespeare had united the virgin daughter Perdita with her beautiful mother, Hermione, through the gracious powers of the crone Paulina, combining all the positive elements of female initiatory myth. In *The Tempest*, he relegates mother and crone to the evil world of the senses and unites the virgin with her father and her male counterpart, as Mozart does in *The Magic Flute*, in which Pamina is taken from her evil mother, the Queen of the Night, and restored to the spiritual guidance of her priestly father. In this last play, Shakespeare clearly opts for the stilling of the passions and the peace of intellect, represented by the wise old man, Prospero. The goal was to move out of the body, away from earth and water, away from the erotic feminine pole. Two thousand years of Christian thought had done its masculinizing work on the preclassical mystery rituals of the earth mother.[26] Sexuality is now considered a state of weakness and of bondage to the maternal eros. Its church is untamed nature, with its bogs and pignuts, and its priest is Caliban, the amoral, sociopathic fish-man from whom Miranda must be rescued and restored to the patriarchal logos.

Caliban, the son of an unholy trinity, is a tempter, a little Satan. He urges Stephano to conquest over the isle, murder, and rape. He pulls the two clowns down into water, then into earth (mire), up to their chins in horse piss, at which Trinculo's nose "is in great indignation." In the swamp of the Great Mother, her dragon-children are born and devoured. Her symbolic animal is the prolific, mud-wallowing sow, and, in fact, Isis appears in ancient art both as a white sow and as a woman riding on a pig, a sacred animal to the Near Eastern goddess cults.[27] As son of the swamp goddess, Caliban leads men into mud and lust, away from the paternal logos that is their spiritual goal. The mire into which they fall is like Virgil's filthy Cocytus and is the sign that they have failed in their initiation, which requires renunciation of sense rewards and sinful intent. They are chased by hounds, which Pletho tells us, in the *Magic Oracles of Zoroaster,* terrify initiates. When the demonic dogs bark, one is supposed to stand fast and ignore them, but Stephano and Trinculo flee, howling. They are drawn downward into the earth and the world of the senses, racked with cramps.

Ariel is not subjected to bogs but has been stuck in a tree by the evil witch. The tree represents the Self, "symbol of the source and goal of the individuation process,"[28] as well as of madness and materialism, the opposite pole of the Self. A flight like Ariel's out of the imprisoning tree is common to archaic religions, in which "flight signifies access to a supernatural mode of being god, magician, spirit."[29] Flying into the sky marks the rise of solar religions and the effacement of the dark night rituals of the underworld in the cave of the mother goddess.[30] The later forms of the mystery religions stress overcoming the body, the world, and the woman in order to join with father spirit. In the rituals, the ego identifies itself with spirit instead of body and is reborn in perfection.[31] Once the woman has been purified and is one with the father's will, she can serve as a proper guide out of the body even as the temporal female guided the soul into the body. The Ariel or Psyche figure that Prospero frees from the wood is as much an anima figure for Prospero as is Miranda. Ariel is also a Mercurius, a virgin hermaphrodite who in itself combines all aspects of the soul. Ariel, or Mercurius, according to Jung, is the way to the Tree of Life and the hidden vessel in which "our Sun rises and sets" (*CW* 9ii,241/379). The spirit is that aspect of Prospero who turns his back on vengeance, opting for mercy and freedom from the material world.

For Ariel, liberation is relatively easy, for he/she has not been bound to the sense world. Ariel is an archetypal image of what Jung called the transcendental function, the Mercurius of the alchemists.[32] The royal party, however, must be torn from appetites and attachments. They are unwilling participants in the Lesser Mysteries, having been immersed in the sea, in a kind of Christian baptism, and achieving a catharsis common to the pagan mysteries. The transformation or sea-change is subjective and inward. Their clothes are not even wet, as we have noted, but are better than new, a sign of their moral improvement. They have traveled from Tunis to Naples, retracing Aeneas's trip in Virgil's *Aeneid* from Carthage to Cumae, a few miles from Naples. The baptismal immersion of the group corresponds to the crossing of the river Styx in the *Aeneid* into the realm of sleep. Everyone except Sebastian and Antonio mysteriously keels over, and even these two speak in "sleepy language," dreaming power-nightmares and foul, libidinous deeds which surface from their unconscious. As does Aeneas, they hear a humming of spirits like the sound of bees, a prelude to awakening, a sound commonly heard by those entering the mystical state.

Like Aeneas, they go through symbolic wanderings, looking for the symbolic lost child—their Self or their state of innocence before the fall. This search all initiates must make, as the initiates of Eleusis searched for Persephone in the Eleusinian mysteries. Ariel, playing harpy, siren, and monster, convicts them of guilt, as in Plutarch's account of pagan rites: a drug is used to drive initiates into a frenzy of contrition and confession of sin. Their awareness of guilt is the first stage of their conversion. Ultimately, they stand charmed, unable to move, as in Themistius's description (*Orationes in Patrem*) of initiates about to enter the pagan temple. Their heads spin and they are unable to take a step. Ariel, that imaginative extension of Prospero, is in charge of the visitors while they sleep, guarding them from the murderous Antonio and Sebastian. King Alonso is given a chance to sleep off his grief, and his good angel, Gonzalo, sleeps beside him. Meanwhile, the real, outside world keeps moving, for there are two temporal realities in this play— the dream world and the ordinary world, as among the Australian aboriginals. Antonio and Sebastian do not sleep beside the others, for they are modern, alienated individualists. These two villains have cut themselves off from the social order and live in the dark solitude of Claudius and Iago.

Antonio regards this heavenly sleep as his opportunity for gain (II,i,294-305), planning that Sebastian will become king and his creature. Control of others is a big issue in *The Tempest*, as it is in *Othello*. Antonio is nothing but greed, a faceless archetype of the brother-killer, without the motivation or pain of a Claudius. As Shakespeare aged, his projections became harsher, while the anima figures grow more credible and complete, as in Cleopatra, Hermione, and Miranda. Antonio is the worst of the Machiavellian "new men." When he looks at the sleeping king, he says Alonso is "no better than the earth he lies upon." Reductionistic nominalism has reached its extreme in Antonio. Sebastian isn't quite as rotten; he'd rather have Antonio kill Alonso, promising him a king's favor if he does. Antonio says, well, kill Gonzalo then, while I kill your brother. Sebastian turns white and temporizes, "O, but one word." At this moment, Ariel freezes the frame and wakes the sleepers just as their murderers rush upon them. Antonio and Sebastian, cowards as well as traitors, stop short and walk around whistling, pretending they were merely guarding the camp.

While the island has brought out the vicious motives of the villains, it has also offered a healing sleep to Alonso, who has cheered up and is again ready to hunt for Ferdinand. His despair has been lifted by Ariel's magic, though it will return, for despair is his particular weakness. Fatuous idealism is Gonzalo's, even though he saw what happened to Prospero back in Milan. The desire for power surfaces in villains; the desire for peace in good men. On this island, unconscious motivation begins to break through into consciousness, and the catalyst is the mysterious island on which they are separate from the predictable world of history represented by Milan and Naples.

The archetypal landscape of *The Tempest* is part sea, part island, part woods, cave and swamps. Club Mud, Stephano and Trinculo probably called it when they got back to Naples. It is the landscape of initiation, where people do field work in self-identification. Shakespeare often puts his heroes in the dark woods or subjects them to shipwreck. Hamlet went through a similar process and afterward behaved like a god, indifferent to duty, fate, or death, except for his brief theatrics at Ophelia's grave. Othello took a boat separate from Desdemona's and endured a storm so severe she thought he was dead. Indeed he was, to her. What is the drowning, or semi-drowning, supposed to teach the hero? What does it teach Ferdinand? Drowning is the rite of initiation, the trip beyond consciousness and ego into death. Probably the early Christians were not delicately touched on the forehead with a priest's damp finger, but held underwater by a wild fundamentalist like John the Baptist until they stopped twitching and turned blue. Then they would be hauled up to choke and gasp out their transformative near-death experience. The shipwreck and near-drowning served Ferdinand as a conversion experience, a sacrament.

Prospero's role as hierophant or high priest of this initiation is too obvious to mention, but the roles of Ferdinand and Miranda have strong links to ancient ritual that may not be so obvious. Ferdinand meets his Beatrice, the Sophia of the ancient mysteries, the Virgin Mary of the Christians, and at once recognizes she is his sacred bride, not like the light women of his past. He asks Miranda, not Prospero, for guidance, for like any wise initiate, he knows his anima guide when he sees her and understands that spiritual marriage is the goal of initiation or enlightenment. He associates Miranda with the morning (III,i), like Hathor the Dawn, and praises her as the lover in the biblical *Song of Songs* praises his bride. She assists him in his ordeals and discipline and accompanies him at the mythic revels, starring Ceres the birth goddess and Iris the Rainbow, who cuts the thread of life.

The first person Ferdinand sees after his descent into the underworld and reawakening on the island is the angelic Miranda. This encounter in nature, away from Ferdinand's usual civilized environment, is a classic meeting of animus and anima figures on the edge of consciousness, on their way to convergence. For him, as for others, Miranda is the island. She is Ceres, the Mother, who will nourish, not tyrannically control. As Hecate, the goddess of the underworld, paradoxically gives birth, the Eleusinian mysteries celebrated the return of Persephone, the young woman who brings nature to life.[33] Everybody wants Miranda/Persephone, just as everybody except modest Ferdinand wants to rule the island. She is the incarnation of Persephone, who births men into life, brings harvests and babies and wonder, while Prospero, her male counterpart, rebirths heroes through initiation, instructing them by plays-within-plays, punishment, intellectual authority, and example. The two must become yoked together as equals, close as the two terms of a metaphor, if Prospero is to unify his own fragmented psyche, as well as Ferdinand's. Early in the play he orders Miranda about, puts her to sleep whenever something interesting is about to happen, and scolds her cruelly: "What, my foot my tutor? One more word and I will chide thee, if not hate thee." As a sympathetic parent, he's not any more a winner than he was as a duke, at least by modern standards. Yet Miranda is ultimately set free to marry Ferdinand, becoming Prospero's equal. He even lets her stay alone with Ferdinand in the cave and was no doubt glad to see the way she caught her fiancé cheating at chess. She's turning into a professor, like her father, though a more good-humored one. Her ordeal by sea as an infant and growing up with Caliban as her only chum were a harsh enough initiation; by the time we see her, Miranda has been prepared for self-realization. The only initiation she now needs is union with her animus, her perfect complement.

When Ferdinand first meets Miranda, she is still a half-conscious child, a sleeping beauty, dependent on her father to tell her who she is. Yet her presence had kept Prospero alive on the dinghy, for she smiled on him with a heavenly fortitude. She is capable of empathy on the scale of Mother Teresa, suffering with those she saw drowning in the wreck. Even divine foreknowledge of events comes to her naturally, for she imagines that "some noble creature" was in the ship. Even now, as we know, Ferdinand is doing a fast, hard Australian crawl straight for the beach. When she sees him, she calls him a thing divine, not merely natural. Up till now, her only suitor was the all-too-natural Caliban, an anagram for Cannibal, in fact, a creature right out of Montaigne's essay, "Of Cannibals." From this rude nature, which eats you alive, Miranda turns to divine art represented by Ferdinand, Eros by daylight. Unlike Psyche or Persephone, Miranda doesn't have to go through the darkness or the underworld before being united with her divine animus. She is already educated by Prospero and experiences self-knowledge as soon as she connects with Ferdinand. At that moment, her Self becomes complete, perfectly integrated and balanced. Only in *The Tempest* and in Harlequin romances is the job so easy. Miranda is immediately so strong and independent that she can bend the rules a bit without losing moral stature, telling Ferdinand her name against her father's wish.

As Prospero well knows, a traitorous, lecherous Caliban lurks in every Ferdinand. In fact, Ferdinand admits to a few rolls in the hay, but swears his soul never got into the act. Unlike Miranda, he must go through an ordeal as part of his initiation. His Caliban side must be disciplined, thus the chaining and log-carrying episode. Besides having enjoyed a bit of nooky at the court, Ferdinand also had some of the swaggering warrior about him. He raises his sword against Prospero, knowing the old man is Miranda's father—not the most tactful way to begin a courtship. Traditional aggressive behavior must drop away for the individuated Self to emerge. Ferdinand and Miranda are not at court; they are in the world of myth, on a sacred island just surfaced out of the unconscious sea. When they go back to Italy, they will take that perfect, father-created island with them, so that they can rule wisely, as Prospero in his youth had not.

Ferdinand is the obedient servant, the noble replacement of brutal Caliban (Act III). As he toils with his logs, Miranda comes up behind him, saying they have three hours safe from Prospero. Already she is an enlightened Desdemona, joined to her animus (a better choice than Othello) and knowing her own mind. She is no weak-kneed Ophelia, but a woman ready to seize the initiative. Ferdinand is barely able to hold onto his log, she's so eager to carry it for him. Miranda in Act III, scene one is the opposite of the proper Renaissance maiden. She offers to do physical labor, defies her father, admits her devotion to her newly met lover, invites him to love her, weeps in obvious compliance with that love, and offers to be his servant if he doesn't want to marry her. Ferdinand doesn't take advantage of her innocence. For him, as for her, love, service, and honesty are unified in his psyche, which is fully individuated the moment he sees her. Because they love each other, he and Miranda make it to wholeness and maturation ahead of Prospero.

The initiate of Eleusis was led into the Great Initiation by a mysterious wise woman, who is both mother and bride. Miranda is not, however, the daughter of Demeter, representative of nature and eros, but of the patriarchy. She is Mary, not Isis, and her power depends on the males who rule her. Her initiation rite is not into a collective frenzy of fertility, but into individuation. The sacred male societies, formed to counter the female control of agricultural mysteries, exalted the individual mind above nature, body, and woman. The male was born of the female but had to slay and transcend her to enter into his father's house, born again of the spirit. In Ferdinand's case, the passage was eased by a mother-bride figure who had herself been born of her father and represented his values. Ferdinand does not have to slay the female dragon because his new father-in-law has already done it; Sycorax is destroyed before the play begins, and the way is clear for entry into the father's cave/grave, from which souls emerge into a new life of the spirit.

Before he led others into initiation, Prospero, the priest-hierophant, had to undergo purgation himself. When Ariel sings the song early in the play about a father lying under the water and going through a sea change, s/he could be describing what happens to Prospero. He moves from thundering judge and magician to humble old man. In short, he learns how to die, to overflow his boundaries and include other selves—not controlling them but accepting them as they are and himself as he is. In Jung's terms, he has completed maturation.

He achieves the last and highest stages of initiation along with Ferdinand and Miranda. For them, at their stage of development, integration means the union of male and female. For Prospero, it is the emergence of a unified Self, that center which Jung says might equally be called "the God within us." Such a figure does not appear in its purity on the stage but is a principle that regulates the interaction between Prospero's ego and the contents of his unconscious. Aspects of it appear in projections, such as Caliban, who represents Prospero's passions. We see Prospero's rage when his masque is interrupted by Caliban's terrorist raid and when he says, "I'll plague them all, even to roaring," not sounding much different from the Caliban he loathes. Throughout the play, Prospero is forced to become more and more aware of his responsibility for his own projections, and ultimately to reabsorb them into himself. As individuation proceeds, the Self becomes a symbol for that marriage of opposites, that conscious union of all one's fragments. It does not make a person selfish or individualistic, as ego does, but transcends such selfishness.

Prospero's first transpersonal function, which he carries off with a good deal of egotism and spite, is his educational one. He is unnecessarily rude to Ariel in the beginning, threatening the sprite with being re-imprisoned in the tree. All Ariel had asked was the date of his release from servitude. Prospero answered him as harshly as if the sprite were Caliban. Ferdinand, who is about to win Miranda, is given a harder time than Antonio. Is it possible Prospero's harshness to Ferdinand carries a hint of jealousy? So the play has been read by those who believe Prospero had more than fatherly feeling for Miranda. Incest as metaphor is a common theme and may be read as an urge for union with the anima, the other self. All these characters, however, can be seen as aspects of Prospero himself; they are not fully rounded, but abstract and without personality. Ferdinand may look like a prince, but he talks like a textbook: "The white cold virgin snow upon my heart abates the ardor of my liver" (IV,i,62-3), probably not Shakespeare's words, but words he allowed to stand. One thing about Ferdinand, he's a quick study. Whatever the jealous pangs Prospero may feel when surrendering his Miranda to the younger man, he accepts Ferdinand's penance and humility. No need to spend a long time educating the boy, when other, more needy students are at hand. Besides, Miranda can be trusted to finish what Prospero started, having been schooled by him for twelve years.

Prospero is fortunate to have two star pupils, since the others in the island classroom are dunces. His pedagogical method is designed to suit their weaknesses. For Ferdinand it was humbling labor, for Caliban, blows and pinches, for the nobles, a phantom feast, straight out of *The Odyssey* and delivered by Ariel wearing a harpy costume, the only time Ariel shows an evil side. Ariel's speech refers to a sort of karmic balance between their crimes and this punishment. Prospero and Miranda starved and so will their tormentors. Alonso, for his part in the treason, has lost his son. Each one is feeling exactly the pain they inflicted on another, a tough way to learn empathy and compassion, but apparently the only way for such hardened characters. An Old Testament justice is being carried out here. An eye for an eye. Prospero means to teach every one of them the consequences of his sins, showing them that even nature has rebelled at their perfidy. Admiring Ariel's pedagogical technique— "a grace it had, devouring. Of my instruction hast thou nothing bated (omitted)" (III,iii,93-106)—Prospero gloats that his enemies are in his power. It is not his most attractive moment.

With at least one of the students, King Alonso, the lesson works. As he suffers from the loss of his son, Alonso has a sudden perception. He hears his sin in the wind and waves. Now he wants to follow Ferdinand to the bottom of the sea, expiating his monstrous, unnatural crime against Prospero. Sebastian and Antonio have learned nothing, but like Macbeth, strike out with their swords. Trinculo and Stephano, meanwhile, are staggering through the island mud holes, led on by Ariel. Perhaps they will never learn anything from their pains, but Caliban does. By the time they find their way to the cave, Caliban's drunken haze has worn off, and he is furious with his erstwhile king. Stephano and Trinculo have given up the quest to kill Prospero and are busy gathering the fine clothes Ariel spread around to tempt them. Caliban rushes from one to the other, reminding them of their purpose. At last he gives up, realizing from this lesson in human weakness that he once had a better master and might again. At the end of the play, he asks pardon and promises to seek for grace. No one in the play except Prospero and the young couple comes off so well as the poor monster.

Prospero in his teaching capacity is a Promethean figure, an "archetypal image of human existence...compelled by his own shortcomings to offend against his environment and his companions in growth."[34] Jung writes that this god-fire or prince-priest "transcends the ego personality" *(CW* 9ii,225/354). In myths, this archetype has a divine wisdom which he can translate into human action. He enlightens those who live in darkness. In his effort to raise others to a level beyond mere survival, he suggests the archetype of "the wise old man," who appears as doctor, magician, priest, grandfather, and is the image of wholeness that "compensates [man's] state of spiritual deficiency by contents designed to fill the gap" *(CW* 9ii,216-396). This figure appears when the individual knows he is at the end of his tether and must make crucial decisions. Such a moment occurs for Prospero toward the end of the play, and he is finally able to represent perfectly the archetype of the Self.

The turning point for Prospero comes about as he presents his young initiates with the mysteries of Eleusis—the phantom figures of Demeter and Kore/Persephone. In the Eleusinian mysteries, the Hierophant showed the neophytes an ear of grain, and at this sight, more than mere gratitude for the harvest was aroused.

> To those who had seen Kore at Eleusis this was no mere metaphor..., but the memento of and encounter in which the goddess of the underworld showed herself in a beatific vision.[35]

The opening of the eyes was the goal of the mysteries, a seeing beyond death itself. The fire of Persephone was a purifying one, announcing the transmutation of a human being to an immortal one.[36] Just as the two young people are shown the vision of sublime fertility, Prospero remembers that he is only a frail human being, an old man capable of forgetting that his servant is coming to murder him. For him, the transformative vision includes awareness of his humanity and mortality.

The crucial moment occurs during the mystery play. By now Prospero's enemies are in his pocket, and he's feeling cocky. Ariel, ever tactful, chooses this moment to ask, "Do you love me Master? No?" (IV,i,53). Prospero is preoccupied, brushes Ariel off with, "Dearly, dearly. Do not approach till thou dost hear me call." As a loving response, this one doesn't quite cut it. Ariel broods a bit and does not speak again till Prospero has his sudden fit of anger, breaking off the mystery play in order to deal with Caliban's rebellion. Miranda has never seen him so angry. What's wrong? On the surface, it's Caliban's sneak attack, but underneath, we see an old man who forgot an essential detail and wonders if his mind may be going. He paces up and down, then turns and gives us the reason for his rage: "Our revels now are ended." Prospero's awareness of mortality is beginning to surface. "My old brain is troubled. Be not disturbed with my infirmity," he says to Ferdinand. You children go into the cave and play (IV,i,175-80). A change has come over him. Instead of supervising the young couple, he walks around thinking about how old and broken he is. At just that moment, in his weakness and awareness of mortality, he invites Ariel's presence.

Ariel has learned a thing or two after dealing with Prospero's ego rages. I would have told you about the conspiracy, Ariel says, "But I feared/Lest I might anger thee." So Prospero almost loses the whole game by failing to gauge Ariel's sensitivity. His irrational response? Another tantrum: "I will plague them all/Even to roaring." The ego and its desire for revenge, his Caliban side, is in full swing.

At the beginning of Act V, Prospero shifts gears. His enemies have been immobilized, turned to stone. He has everybody where a man like Othello would want them. Not until the enemy is stone dead can the little ego be safe. Ariel describes their tears and says that Prospero would feel tender if he actually saw them. But Prospero doesn't have to see his conquered enemies. His Ariel side has seen them for him. He actually asks Ariel for advice about whether or not his heart should soften. And Ariel answers, "Mine would, sir, were I human." Prospero then says the words that end his islandlike isolation from other human beings: "And mine shall...Yet with my nobler reason 'gainst my fury/Do I take part, the rarer action is/In virtue than in vengeance" (V, i,22-37). He realizes that all he wanted was their penitence, perhaps for their own sakes more than his. His ego must be dethroned and put in its place. "In hermetic texts this is often depicted as the old king being boiled naked in an alchemical vessel."[37] Individuation, Jung writes, starts with facing the shadow: "The integration of the shadow, or the realization of the personal unconscious, marks the first stage in the analytic process and without it a recognition of anima and animus is impossible" (CW 9ii,22/42). Having acknowledged his shadow, united with his anima, and achieved his individuation, Prospero ends his teaching role and allows his students to be themselves. He has integrated Old Testament justice with New Testament mercy.

In between, he echoes Virgil's troubled, storm-beset hero Aeneas, but Virgil's hero is like John Wayne—never so much as blows his nose. Prospero has an ordinary old man's humanity that Aeneas shows only with a rare ritual gesture. Perhaps Prospero's humble humanity comes out of Shakespeare's reading of Montaigne, who criticized Renaissance humanism and idealism as hopelessly unrealistic. For Prospero, divine grace will be needed to wrap up the loose ends of leadership and make a good exit. He knows that self-knowledge continues until death. No magic wand or Machiavellian scheme will do the job, only the mastered Self. Only the leader who can control himself can guide others.

Immediately afterwards he abjures his rough magic, drowns his book, breaks his staff, and puts on his court clothes. The words he says to wake the penitents are as gentle as if he were singing them, in echo of Themistius' account of the Eleusinian mysteries. Themistius writes that after the hierophant opens the temple door to the confused initiates, "the mist and thick cloud were dispersed, and the mind (of the initiates) emerged from the depth, full of brightness and light in place of the previous darkness." They moved from the water or mist into air, or allegorically, out of purgatory into Elysium, the terrestrial paradise. Shakespeare uses similar words to describe the waking of the entranced nobles: "The charm dissolves apace/And as the morning steals upon the night/ Melting the darkness, so their rising senses/Begin to chase the ignorant fumes that mantle/Their clearer reason" (V,i,71-75). As he wakes the sleepers, he frees Ariel, admitting freely that he will miss the spirit. The new Prospero has no trouble expressing love. He even forgives his brother, the villain who like Iago at the end says nothing.

Alonso, having learned repentance, carries his learning even further when Prospero tells him Ferdinand is certainly dead and to bear the loss in patience. The king wishes he himself had drowned, if his death could mean that his son might live. "Greater love than this has no man, that he lays down his life for his friend," Jesus said. When Prospero sees Alonso's grief, and then his joy at meeting Ferdinand and Miranda, he becomes as gentle as a parent to Alonso: "There sir, stop. Let us not burden our remembrance with a heaviness that's gone." As Alonso is cured of his despair, Prospero is cured of his desire for revenge. As Prospero accepts and forgives others, he becomes whole.

Ferdinand and Miranda, symbols for integration, are before our eyes, playing the chess game, symbolically the game of life, which they have learned from a master. They know it is an illusion, yet take their role with loving responsibility. They are prepared to go back to Naples/ Milan and take on the rule of both, even knowing that the Antonios, the snakes, are in the garden. Once Miranda, who has carried the value of the soul and of feminine relatedness throughout the play, has united with Ferdinand, Prospero can internalize his feeling function.[38] By giving up his magic as he gives up Miranda, Prospero has freed them to take on their new roles as rulers. As for Prospero, he does not mourn his loss, but only asks for his freedom. He no longer depends on magic, but humbly on grace. Like the characters being folded into his cave, he wants to be folded into God. He is no longer an island.

Only one step toward inclusiveness and complete integration remains. Caliban skulks in, shivering and moaning that he'll be pinched to death. Prospero suggests that Alonso take responsibility for his own drunken servants, then reaches out to Caliban, saying with perhaps more fondness than sternness, "This thing of darkness, I acknowledge mine." Now, he says, nothing is perceived as other than Self. Even the savage is redeemed and integrated. Acknowledging his dark side is the key to integration. Like the professor he is, Prospero takes responsibility for his failed student, at last admitting that he *himself* is Caliban, son of furious Sycorax. In doing so, he turns the educational experiment into a success for both of them. The conjunction of opposites is complete. At the end, Prospero ushers all the characters into the cave, signifying that he has transcended all boundaries, integrated all parts of himself.

To go through the fiery ring into the aether is to risk and transcend death and to enter spiritual ecstasy. The *mystes*, or initiate of Eleusis, removed her veil when she came to the fire, marking the shift from dark to full light. The primitive form of the mysteries was the reaping rite of Persephone's loss and return, which in time became a metaphor of interior transformation. The primitive form, featuring the grain, was represented in the Lesser Mysteries of Eleusis, while the inner transformation was part of the "inner ritual or psychological cohesion of the Mystery action."[39] Initiates lived through the death and return of the daughter to the sorrowing mother, as Christians live through the death of Jesus, his resurrection and return to Mary. As in the mystery religions, our material life is a sleep, a dream, and we wake to reality only after death. Ferdinand enters the cave, a place consecrated to the gods in myth. The Indo-European *kevo*, meaning to swell, be pregnant, also means cave, while the Latin *arca* (cell, cave) is directly related to arcana or mysteries (*CW* 5,373/579). The cave is a funeral urn, out of which the soul is born into its next state,[40] which in Prospero's case is death. The cave is also a *sancta sanctorum*, the Judeo-Christian holy of holies, where Gonzalo wishes to "drop a blessed crown" on the couple. Perhaps Shakespeare means both a temporal crown and the one given to the fully initiated, to the Christian saint in heaven. Prospero has a "second life," and he is reborn into revelation, as is the participant in the Greater Initiation, who goes from death to life, from bondage to liberation.

From the neolithic community ritual that celebrated the sprouting of the grain, the mysteries historically became a sacred initiation for a privileged few. With the coming of the modern era and Shakespeare's *Tempest*, "consciousness now faces inward and becomes aware of the Self, about which the ego revolves in a perpetual paradox of identity and non-identity."[41] From the ancient god-king, who represented a collective soul consumed in a ritual feast by members, a new order of initiates has arisen. Each of us is a sacred Self/King. Each of us, through death and rebirth, can become Osiris, Christ, God.[42] The risk, of course, is ego inflation, that is, mistaking the ego for the Self, and thus falling back into the mother-swamp of emotion, as Prospero is almost overcome by his bitch aspect. Like Caliban, he is almost drawn back into the bog of unconsciousness, in which subject and object are one. Jung points out, "The West is always seeking uplift, but the East seeks a sinking or deepening...into the maternal depths of nature" (*CW* 11,570/936). Caliban and his mother represent that aspect of the East that an individuated Westerner such as Prospero must acknowledge but not allow to overcome him.

Like all of us born in the West, according to Jung, Prospero must accept the ongoing conflict between two psychic poles, a conflict which is expressed in symbols, of which Shakespeare's tempest is one. The analyst must know these symbols in order to assist at the union of conscious ('male') and unconscious ('female') contents of the psyche, in Jung's "transcendent function." Prospero gathers all the pieces of himself, good and bad, word and image, into his home, his cave, his metaphoric funerary urn, acknowledging them as his own. When Prospero drowns his book and lays aside his magic mantle, he is both godlike in his moral power and human in his weakness. The opposites do not dissolve as they conjoin, but maintain both their identity and their polar relationship, while the Self is painfully conscious of their uneasy coexistence.

Even while Prospero celebrates the nuptials of Ferdinand and Miranda, his mind is on his death. In Milan, he says mournfully, every "third thought shall be my grave." His life has been both "solemn temple" and "insubstantial pageant," and he must accept as equally real or unreal both his consciousness and his dissolution. His very Self is both known and unknown, human and animal, divine and mortal. Only death will set him free of dichotomy. Until he dies, Prospero will be the alchemical hermaphrodite, standing on the dragon but with the crown of the integrated Self hanging over his head. He models Neumann's future human being, who accepts both individuation and unity with all men in the collective unconscious.

> A future humanity will realize the center, which the individual personality today experiences as his own self-center, to be one with humanity's very self.[43]

Notes

Introduction

1. All *CW* references are to *The Collected Works of C. G. Jung* (Princeton, N. J.: Princeton University Press, 1953-1979). References are to volume, page, and paragraph numbers.

2. T. S. Eliot, *The Use of Poetry and the Use of Criticism* (London: Faber and Faber, 1933).

3. Maud Bodkin, *Archetypal Patterns in Poetry* (London: Oxford University Press, 1934), p. 8.

4. Charles Lyons, *Shakespeare and the Ambiguity of Love's Triumph* (The Hague: Mouton, 1971), p. 12.

5. John Holloway, *The Story of the Night: Studies in Shakespeare's Major Tragedies* (Lincoln, Neb.: University of Nebraska Press, 1966), p. 177.

6. Ernest Kris with Abraham Kaplan, "Aesthetic Ambiguity" in *Psychoanalytic Explorations in Art* (New York: International Universities Press, 1952), pp. 252-253.

Hamlet

1. Jacques Lacan, "Hamlet," *Yale French Studies* (1978).

2. Ralph Berry, *The Shakespearean Metaphor* (London: Macmillan, 1978), pp. 62-63.

3. Alessandro Serpieri, "Reading the Signs: Toward a Semiotics of Shakespearean Drama," in *Alternative Shakespeares*, ed. J. Drakakis (London: Methuen, 1985), p. 111.

4. Donald W. Winnicott, "Creativity and Its Origins," in *Playing and Reality* (London: Tavistock, 1971); André Green, *Hamlet et Hamlet, une interpretation psychoanalytique de la representation* (Paris: Ballard, 1982), p. 256.

5. Lacan, *op. cit.*, p. 18.

6. J. F. MacCannell quotes Lacan in *Figuring Lacan: Criticism and the Cultural Unconscious* (Lincoln, Neb.: University of Nebraska Press, 1986), p. 90.

7. W. H. Clemen, *The Development of Shakespearean Imagery* (Cambridge, Mass.: Harvard University Press, 1951), pp. 227-229.

8. Lacan, *op. cit.*, p. 47.

9. Maynard Mack, "The World of Hamlet," *Yale Review*, XLI (1952), pp. 502-523.

10. Edward Edinger, "Outline of Analytical Psychology," *Quadrant* (Spring, 1968), p. 12; Jung, *CW* 8, 157/339.

11. Lacan, *op. cit.*, p. 36.

12. J. Rose, "Sexuality in the Reading of Shakespeare," *Alternative Shakespeares*, p. 41.

13. J. Rose, "Hamlet, the *Mona Lisa* of Literature," *Critical Quarterly*, (Spring/Summer, 1986), p. 28.

14. Erich Neumann, *Art and the Creative Unconscious*, tr. Ralph Manheim, Bollingen Series LXI (Princeton, N. J.: Princeton University Press, 1959), p. 185.

15. Serpieri, *op. cit.*, pp. 123-125.

16. Alex Aronson, *Psyche and Symbol in Shakespeare* (Bloomington, Ind.: Indiana University Press, 1972), p. 26.

17. Erik Erikson, *Identity: Youth and Crisis* (New York: Norton, 1968), p. 240.

18. James Hillman, *A Blue Fire,* ed. Thomas Moore (New York: Harper and Row, 1989), p. 227.

19. *Ibid.*

20. James Hillman, *op. cit.*, p. 236; for *puer* material in general, I am indebted to Michael Howard, Ph.D., of Pacifica Graduate Institute.

21. Aronson, p. 248.

22. Berry, p. 72.

23. James Hillman, *Re-Visioning Psychology* (New York: Harper and Row, 1975), p. 109; Miguel de Unamuno, *The Tragic Sense of Life*, tr. J. E. C. Flitch (New York: Dover, 1954), p. 69.

24. H. D. F. Kitto, *Form and Meaning in Drama* (London: Methuen, 1956), p. 327.

Othello

1. Marion Woodman, *The Pregnant Virgin* (Toronto: Inner City Books, 1985), p. 48.

2. Leslie Fiedler, *The Stranger in Shakespeare* (New York: Stein and Day, 1972), p. 174.

3. Christine Downing, *The Goddess: Mythological Images of the Feminine* (New York: Crossroad, 1987), p. 61.

4. Woodman, *op. cit.*, pp. 45-46.

5. Marie-Louise von Franz, *Alchemy: An Introduction to the Symbolism and the Psychology* (Toronto: Inner City Books, 1980), p. 127.

6. Woodman, *op. cit.*, p. 36.

7. Erich Neumann, *The Origins and History of Consciousness* , tr. R. F. C. Hull (Princeton, N. J.: Princeton University Press, 1970), p. 353.

8. Leslie Fiedler, *op. cit.*, p. 147.

9. C. G. Jung and Carl Kerenyi, *Essays on a Science of Mythology*, Bollingen Series XXII (Princeton, N. J.: Princeton University Press, 1963), p. 129.

10. Daniel Weiss, *The Critic Agonistes* (Seattle: University of Washington Press, 1985), p. 25.

11. Woodman, *op. cit.*, p. 128.

12. Woodman, *op. cit.*, p. 170.

13. Hillman, *Insearch* (New York: Charles Scribner's Sons, 1967), p. 81.

14. Hillman, *op. cit.*, p. 105.

The Tempest

1. James Hillman, "Peaks and Vales," in *Puer Papers* (Dallas: Spring Publications, 1979), p. 56.

2. James Hillman, *Re-Visioning Psychology*, p. x.

3. Neil Cobb, *Prospero's Island* (London: Coventure, 1984), p. 72.

4. Marie-Louise von Franz and James Hillman, *Jung's Typology* (Dallas: Spring Publications, 1971), p. 54.

5. Fiedler, *The Stranger in Shakespeare*, pp. 232ff.

6. Marie-Louise von Franz, *Shadow and Evil in Fairy Tales* (Dallas: Spring Publications, 1974), p. 106.

7. Cobb, p. 87.

8. James Hillman, *A Blue Fire*, pp. 220-228.

9. Neumann, *The Origins and History of Consciousness*, p. 352.

10. C. G. Jung, *Memories, Dreams, Reflections*, ed. Aniela Jaffe, tr. R. and C. Winston (New York: Vintage, 1965), p. 335.

11. Hippolytus, *Elenchos*, VIII, 12, 5ff, cited in *CW* 9,ii, 218/340.

12. Aronson, *op. cit.*, p. 206.

13. Joseph Summers, *Dreams of Love and Power* (Oxford: Clarendon Press, 1984), p. 139; Joseph Henderson, "Symbolism of the Unconscious in Two Plays of Shakespeare," in *The Well-Tended Tree*, ed. Hilda Kirsch (New York: Putnam and C. G. Jung Foundation for Analytical Psychology, 1971), pp. 289-292.

14. G. Wilson Knight, *The Crown of Life* (London: Oxford University Press, 1947), p. 215.

15. Ernst Kantoriwicz, *The King's Two Bodies* (Princeton, N. J.: Princeton University Press, 1957), *passim*.

16. Knight, *op. cit.*, p. 228.

17. Knight, *op. cit.*, p. 243.

18. Aronson, *op. cit.*, p. 271.

19. Colin Still, *The Timeless Theme* (London: Ivor Nicholson and Watson, Ltd., 1936), p. 22; n. 1 on p. 27.

20. Still, *op. cit.*, p. 22.

21. C. G. Jung (Basel: Seminar, Oct. 1934, privately printed, 1935), p. 84.

22. Still, *op. cit.*, p. 135.

23. Lucian, "The Downward Journey," *Works of Lucian,* ed. and tr. A. M. Harmon (Cambridge, Mass.: Harvard University Press, 1968), vol. 2, p. 43.

24. Cobb, p. 32; n. on p. 92.

25. Joseph Campbell, *The Masks of God: Creative Mythology* (New York: Penguin, 1968), p. 17.

26. Rachel Levy, *European Religious Conceptions of the Stone Age* (New York: Harper and Row, 1963), *passim.*

27. *Eleusinian and Bacchic Mysteries,* ed. J. Weitstein (Amsterdam, n. d.), p. 24.

28. Aronson, *op. cit.,* p. 206.

29. Mircea Eliade, *The Sacred and the Profane,* tr. Willard Trask (New York: Harcourt, Brace and World, 1959), p. 176.

30. Eliade, *op. cit.,* p. 158.

31. Neumann, *The Origins and History of Consciousness,* pp. 254-255.

32. Cobb, 55.

33. C. Kerenyi, *Eleusis: Archetypal Image of Mother and Daughter,* tr. Ralph Manheim, Bollingen Series (New York: Pantheon Books, 1967), p. 93.

34. C. Kerenyi, *Promethus: Archetypal Image of Human Existence,* tr. Ralph Manheim (London: Thames and Hudson, 1963), p. 55.

35. C. Kerenyi, *Eleusis,* p. 94.

36. *Op. cit.,* pp. 102-103.

37. Cobb, p. 42.

38. *Op. cit.,* p. 152.

39. Kerenyi, *Eleusis,* p. 120.

40. Eliade, *op. cit.,* p. 179.

41. Neumann, *The Origins and History of Consciousness,* pp. 255-256.

42. Neumann, *op. cit.,* p. 428.

43. Neumann, *op. cit.,* p. 418.

Works Cited

Aronson, Alex. *Psyche and Symbol in Shakespeare*. Bloomington, Ind.: Indiana University Press, 1972.

Berry, Ralph. *The Shakespearean Metaphor*. London: Macmillan, 1978.

Bodkin, Maud. *Archetypal Patterns in Poetry*. London: Oxford University Press, 1934.

Bradley, A. C. *Shakespearean Tragedy*. New York: St. Martin's Press, 1960.

Campbell, Joseph. *The Masks of God: Creative Mythology*. New York: Penguin, 1968.

Clemen, W. H. *The Development of Shakespearean Imagery*. Cambridge, Mass.: Harvard University Press, 1951.

Cobb, Neil. *Prospero's Island*. London: Coventure, 1984.

Derrida, Jacques. *Of Grammatology*. G. Spivak, tr. Paris: Minuit, 1967.

Downing, Christine. *The Goddess: Mythological Images of the Feminine*. New York: Crossroads, 1987.

Eliade, Mircea. *The Sacred and the Profane*. Willard Trask, tr. New York: Harcourt, Brace and World, 1959.

Eliot, T. S. *The Use of Poetry and the Use of Criticism..* London: Faber and Faber, 1933.

Erikson, Erik. *Identity: Youth and Crisis*. New York: Norton, 1968.

Fiedler, Leslie. *The Stranger in Shakespeare*. New York: Stein and Day, 1972.

Franz, Marie-Louise von. *Alchemy: An Introduction to the Symbolism and the Psychology*. Toronto: Inner City Books, 1980.

Hillman, James. *A Blue Fire*. Thomas Moore, ed. New York: Harper and Row, 1989.

Hillman, James. *Re-Visioning Psychology*. New York: Harper and Row, 1975.

Holloway, John. *The Story of the Night: Studies in Shakespeare's Major Tragedies*. Lincoln, Neb.: University of Nebraska Press, 1966.

Jung, C. G. *Collected Works*. New York: Bollingen, 1966.

_____. *Memories, Dreams, Reflections*. Aniela Jaffe, ed., R. and C. Winston, tr. New York: Vintage, 1965.

Kantorowicz, E. *The King's Two Bodies*. Princeton, N. J.: Princeton University Press, 1957.

Kerenyi, C. *Eleusis: Archetypal Image of Mother and Daughter*. Ralph Manheim, tr. New York: Pantheon, 1967.

_____. *Prometheus: Archetypal Image of Human Existence*. Ralph Manheim, tr. London: Thames and Hudson, 1963.

Kerenyi, C., and Jung, C. G. *Essays on a Science of Mythology*. Princeton, N. J.: Princeton University Press, 1963.

Kitto, H. D. F. *Form and Meaning in Drama*. London: Methuen, 1956.

Knight, G. Wilson. *The Crown of Life*. London: Oxford University Press, 1947.

Leavis, F. R. "Diabolic Intellect and the Noble Hero: or the Sentimentalist's Othello," in *The Common Pursuit*. New York: New York University Press, 1952.

Levy, Rachel. *European Religious Conceptions of the Stone Age*. New York: Harper and Row, 1963.

Lyons, Charles. *Shakespeare and the Ambiguity of Love's Triumph*. The Hague: Mouton, 1971.

MacCannell, J. F. *Figuring Lacan: Criticism and the Cultural Unconscious*. Lincoln, Neb.: University of Nebraska Press, 1986.

Neumann, Erich. *The Origins and History of Consciousness*. R. F. C. Hull, tr. Princeton, N. J.: Princeton University Press, 1970.

_____. *Art and the Creative Unconscious*. Ralph Manheim, tr. Princeton, N. J.: Princeton University Press, 1959.

Still, Colin. *The Timeless Theme*. London: Ivor Nicholson and Watson, Ltd., 1936.

Summers, Joseph. *Dreams of Love and Power*. Oxford: Clarendon Press, 1984.

Unamuno, Miguel. *The Tragic Sense of Life*. J. E. C. Flitch, tr. New York: Dover, 1954.

Weiss, Daniel. *The Critic Agonistes*. Seattle: University of Washington Press, 1985.

Woodman, Marion. *The Pregnant Virgin*. Toronto: Inner City Books, 1985.

Index

adaptation, 67, 80
Aeneas, 96, 105
aesthetics, 2, 77
alchemy, 83
ambivalence, 14, 26, 45, 48
anima, 13, 18, 27, 42-46, 49, 52,
    57, 62-63, 65-66, 70-72, 74,
    84, 86, 94, 96-99, 102, 105
animus, 43-47, 53, 68, 71, 84,
    86-88, 99-100, 105
archetype, 3-5, 13, 19, 27-29, 43,
    45, 47, 76-79, 83-84, 89, 97,
    103
Artemis, 49
autonomous complex, 2
Avalon, 90

Bradley, 1, 40

castration, 13
cave, 93
Christ, Christian, 19, 75, 83, 90-
    92, 95-96, 98, 106-107
Cocytus, 95
Coleridge, 20
collective unconscious, 1, 2, 29,
    108
commerce, 59-60
conjunction of opposites, 29, 106
consciousness, 2, 4, 16, 27, 36,
    44, 72, 74, 77, 80-81, 85-86,
    90, 93, 98-99, 107
creation, 1, 9, 31

Dante, 1, 91
deconstruction, 40
Dee, Dr. John, 77
Demeter, 47, 81, 101, 103
Derrida, 25, 40
Dido, 85
Dionysius, 29, 46
dragon, 8, 95, 101, 108
drowning, 37, 57, 87, 98-99
dulcis et utile, 84

ego, 3, 6, 17-19, 21, 27-29, 33,
    35, 41, 43, 48-52, 54, 66, 70,
    72, 75, 101
ego-inflation, 80, 107
elements, 90, 95
Eleusinian mysteries, 91-92, 97,
    99, 103, 105
Eliot, T. S., 1, 8, 17
Elysium, 90, 97
empiricism, 76-77
entropy, 12, 35
Erikson, 28
Eros, 27, 53, 65, 84, 100

feminine, 8, 21, 26-28, 35, 39-40,
    42, 56-58, 63, 76, 78, 81, 84,
    89, 92, 94- 95, 106
Freud, 6-9, 12-13, 26, 36, 40

Galahad, 23
Gilgamesh, 47, 51, 74
Great Mother, 26, 28, 81, 95

Hades, 46-47, 56, 61, 70, 88
harmony, 23, 39, 51, 78, 93
Hecate, 19, 32, 36
hierophant, 97-98, 101
Hillman, 37, 74, 76
humors, 23

images, 1-2, 7, 45, 76, 90, 94
imagination, 42, 45, 77, 84, 93
incest, 33, 44, 47, 74, 85
individualism, 4, 69, 89
individuation, 3, 22, 27-28, 43,
    46, 86, 88, 95, 101, 105, 108
initiation, 4, 20, 47, 74, 79, 83,
    88, 90- 92, 95, 98, 99-101, 107
integration, 21, 37, 39, 43, 53,
    59, 63, 78, 105-106
island, 60, 80-81, 85-86, 89, 92-
    94, 98-100, 102-104, 106

Jones, 6, 17, 32, 36

www.ingramcontent.com/pod-product-compliance
Lightning Source LLC
Chambersburg PA
CBHW050220270326
41914CB00003BA/499